Freedom Press

M203 : 40-MM GRENADE LAUNCHER

They are provided for informational purposes only.

ISBN-13: 978-1511502573
ISBN-10: 1511502576

FAIR USE ASSERTION

40-MM
GRENADE LAUNCHER,
M203

FEBRUARY 2003

FIELD MANUAL
NO. 3-22.31

HEADQUARTERS
DEPARTMENT OF THE ARMY
Washington, DC, 13 February 2003

40-MM GRENADE LAUNCHER, M203

CONTENTS

DISTRIBUTION RELEASE: Approved for public release; distribution is unlimited.

---

*This publication supersedes FM 23-31, 20 September 1994, and rescinds
DA Form 2946-R, July 1974.

PREFACE

This manual provides technical information on and training and combat techniques for the M203 grenade launcher. Intended users include leaders and designated grenadiers, who will use this information to successfully integrate the M203 into their combat operations. This manual discusses gunnery training and train-the-trainer and includes an appendix on the 40-mm grenade launcher, M79.

The tactical positions shown in this manual were drawn to enhance the reader's understanding of related subject material and are *not* tactically correct.

Unless stated otherwise, masculine nouns and pronouns in this publication do not refer exclusively to men.

The proponent of this publication is the United States Army Infantry School. Send comments and recommendations on DA Form 2028 (Recommended Changes to Publications and Blank Forms) directly to Commandant, United States Army Infantry School, ATTN: ATSH-ATD, Fort Benning, GA 31905-5595 or send an email to doctrine@benning.army.mil.

CHAPTER 1
INTRODUCTION

This chapter discusses the training strategy and combat conditions for the 40-mm grenade launcher, M203. (Appendix A discusses the M79 model.)

1-1. TRAINING STRATEGY

An effective overall training strategy produces well-trained grenadiers and trainers by integrating resources into an effective year-round training program. Beginning with IET and continuing both in other institutions (NCOES, IOBC, and IOAC) and in the unit, such a program trains and sustains the individual and collective skills needed to perform the wartime mission. Specific training strategies are implemented by institutional and unit training programs, and supporting training strategies are implemented through the use of other resources such as publications, ranges, ammunition, training aids, devices, simulators, and simulations. The year-round program includes periodic preliminary marksmanship training followed by zeroing and range qualification firing. Other key elements of the program are training for the trainers and refresher training for nonfiring skills. The example in Figure 1-1 on page 1-3 shows the flow of unit sustainment training.

a. **Institutional Training**. Training strategy begins with combat arms initial-entry training (IET), which trains soldiers in the standards of M203 gunnery tasks. Soldiers graduate with basic and advanced M203 skills that include maintaining the M203 and using it to hit a variety of targets. Other institutional training programs, such as NCOES, IOBC, and IOAC, reinforce these skills. Related soldier skills are integrated into tactical training (STP 21-1-SMCT).

b. **Unit Training**. Training continues in units, where, in addition to sustaining proficiency in skills gained in institutional training, leaders and soldiers develop and sustain new skills such as suppressive and supporting fire. These skills are integrated into collective training exercises to develop combat readiness. Preliminary marksmanship training is conducted before firings and as other opportunities arise. (Appendix B discusses an M203 unit training program.) To be effective, a unit training program focuses on three battlefield variables:

(1) *Target*. Is the target moving or stationary, single or multiple?

(2) *Grenadier*. Is the grenadier moving or stationary? Is he kneeling, prone, or standing?

(3) *Conditions*. Is visibility full or limited? Must soldiers wear protective masks or not? Is it day or night?

c. **Initial and Sustainment Training**. A task that is taught correctly and learned well is retained longer, so initial training is critical. In addition to being more easily sustained, well-trained skills are also easier to regain if not used for some time. Retraining may be needed, however, if too much time elapses, if training doctrine changes, or if personnel turnover is high.

(1) *Collective Training*. Collective training exercises progress from drills (squad, section, and platoon) to STXs, and then to live-fire tactical exercises (LFXs). Drill books

and MTPs provide tasks and guidance needed to plan and conduct the exercises. After each, leaders and trainers conduct an AAR to evaluate both individual and unit proficiency. The results provide readiness indicators and requirements for future training. LFXs provide leaders with an overview of unit proficiency and training effectiveness. They can be conducted on any range approved for M203 firing.

(2) *Leader Training*. The most critical part of the Army's overall gunnery training strategy is to train the trainers and leaders first. Leader courses, however, include only limited M203 training, so officers and NCOs should use available publications to develop their proficiency with the M203. Publications help leaders plan, conduct, and evaluate their gunnery training programs. Proponent schools provide training support materials (field manuals, training aids, devices, simulators, and audiovisual programs), which provide the doctrinal foundations for training the force.

(3) *Advanced Training*. Once the soldier knows the weapon and has demonstrated skill in zeroing, training strategy provides for additional live-fire training and target-acquisition exercises, which are conducted at various ranges. To develop proficiency, soldiers must master different types of targets and scenarios of increasing difficulty.

(4) *Proficiency Assessment*. This is conducted on the zeroing and record live-fire exercise range when soldiers complete IET.

1-2. COMBAT CONDITIONS

The trainer must realize that qualification is not an end but a step toward reaching combat readiness. To reach combat readiness, the grenadier should consider his position, the capabilities of his weapon, and the following combat conditions:

a. Enemy personnel are seldom visible except when assaulting.

b. Most combat fire must be directed at an area where the enemy has been detected or is suspected but cannot be seen. Area targets consist of objects or outlines of men irregularly spaced along covered and concealed areas (ground folds, hedges, borders of woods).

c. Most combat targets can be detected by smoke, flash, dust, noise, or movement and are visible only for a moment.

d. Some combat targets can be engaged by using reference points, predetermined fire, or range card data.

e. The nature of the target and irregularities of terrain and vegetation may require a grenadier to use a variety of positions to place effective fire on the target. In a defensive situation, the grenadier usually fires from a supported fighting position.

f. Most combat targets have a low-contrast outline and are obscured. Therefore, choosing an aiming point in elevation is difficult.

g. Time-stressed fire in combat can be divided into three types:
- A single, fleeing target that must be engaged quickly.
- Area targets engaged within the time they remain available.
- A surprise target that must be engaged at once with instinctive, accurate fire.

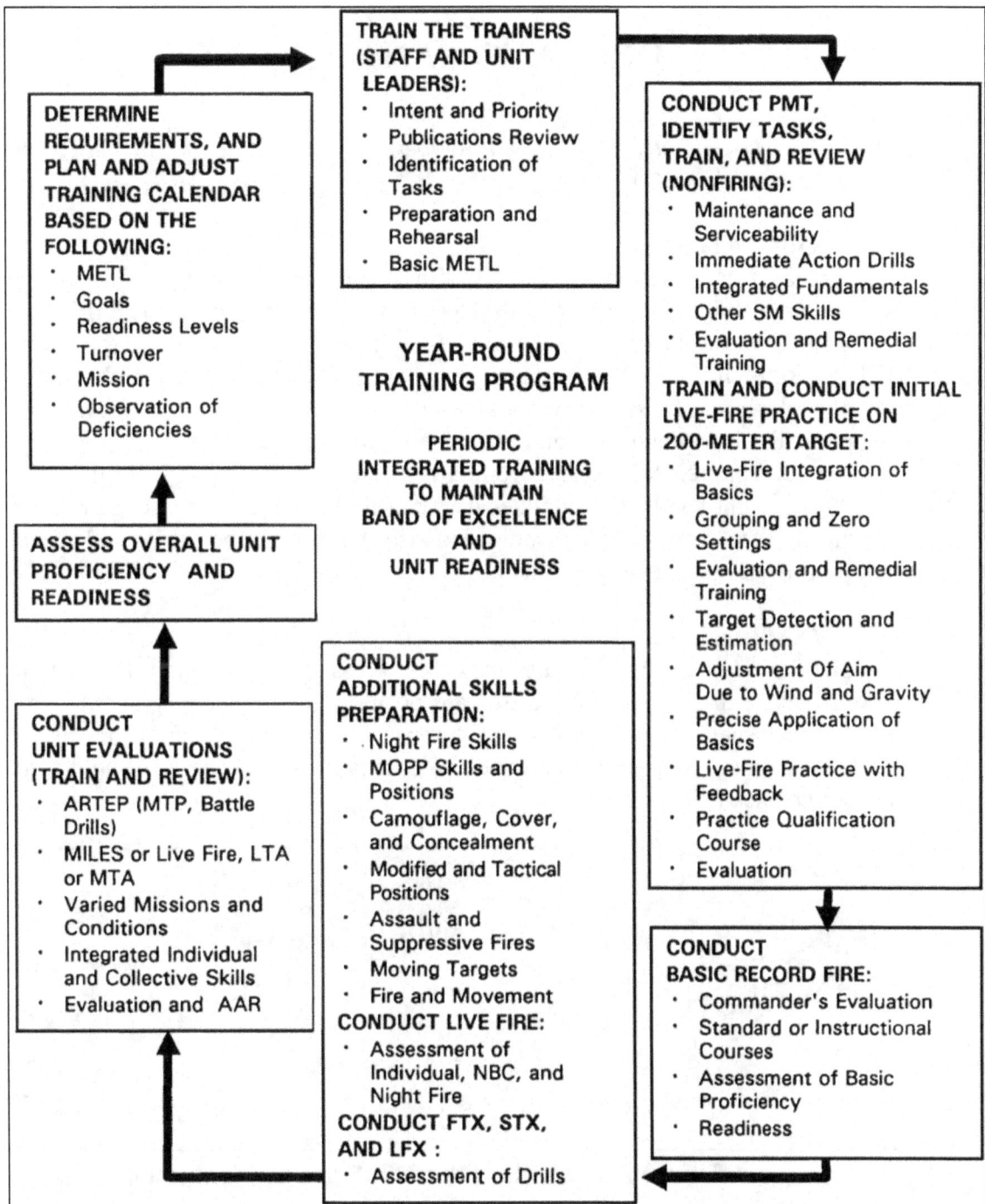

DETERMINE REQUIREMENTS, AND PLAN AND ADJUST TRAINING CALENDAR BASED ON THE FOLLOWING:
- METL
- Goals
- Readiness Levels
- Turnover
- Mission
- Observation of Deficiencies

TRAIN THE TRAINERS (STAFF AND UNIT LEADERS):
- Intent and Priority
- Publications Review
- Identification of Tasks
- Preparation and Rehearsal
- Basic METL

YEAR-ROUND TRAINING PROGRAM

PERIODIC INTEGRATED TRAINING TO MAINTAIN BAND OF EXCELLENCE AND UNIT READINESS

CONDUCT PMT, IDENTIFY TASKS, TRAIN, AND REVIEW (NONFIRING):
- Maintenance and Serviceability
- Immediate Action Drills
- Integrated Fundamentals
- Other SM Skills
- Evaluation and Remedial Training

TRAIN AND CONDUCT INITIAL LIVE-FIRE PRACTICE ON 200-METER TARGET:
- Live-Fire Integration of Basics
- Grouping and Zero Settings
- Evaluation and Remedial Training
- Target Detection and Estimation
- Adjustment Of Aim Due to Wind and Gravity
- Precise Application of Basics
- Live-Fire Practice with Feedback
- Practice Qualification Course
- Evaluation

ASSESS OVERALL UNIT PROFICIENCY AND READINESS

CONDUCT UNIT EVALUATIONS (TRAIN AND REVIEW):
- ARTEP (MTP, Battle Drills)
- MILES or Live Fire, LTA or MTA
- Varied Missions and Conditions
- Integrated Individual and Collective Skills
- Evaluation and AAR

CONDUCT ADDITIONAL SKILLS PREPARATION:
- Night Fire Skills
- MOPP Skills and Positions
- Camouflage, Cover, and Concealment
- Modified and Tactical Positions
- Assault and Suppressive Fires
- Moving Targets
- Fire and Movement

CONDUCT LIVE FIRE:
- Assessment of Individual, NBC, and Night Fire

CONDUCT FTX, STX, AND LFX :
- Assessment of Drills

CONDUCT BASIC RECORD FIRE:
- Commander's Evaluation
- Standard or Instructional Courses
- Assessment of Basic Proficiency
- Readiness

Figure 1-1. Unit gunnery sustainment strategy.

CHAPTER 2
OPERATION AND FUNCTION

This chapter discusses the operation and function of the M203 grenade launcher.

2-1. OPERATION

The grenadier's operations include loading, unloading, and firing the weapon. The weapon uses a high-low propulsion system to fire a 40-mm round. The firing pin strikes the primer, whose flash ignites the propellant in the brass powder-charge cup inside the high-pressure chamber. The burning propellant produces 35,000 psi chamber pressure, which ruptures the brass powder-charge cup at the vent holes and allows the gases to escape to the low-pressure chamber in the cartridge case. There the pressure drops to 3,000 psi and propels the grenade from the muzzle at a velocity of 250 fps. The grenade's 37,000-rpm right-hand spin stabilizes it during flight and applies enough rotational force to arm the fuze. The weapon is unloaded with the barrel open and fired from a closed bolt. It must be cocked before it can be placed on SAFE.

2-2. LOADING

To load the weapon, the grenadier must first press the barrel latch and slide the barrel forward. Once the barrel is in the forward position, the grenadier places the weapon on SAFE and visually inspects the barrel to ensure it is clear. Then he inserts clean, dry, undented ammunition into the chamber and slides the barrel rearward until it locks with an audible click (Figure 2-1).

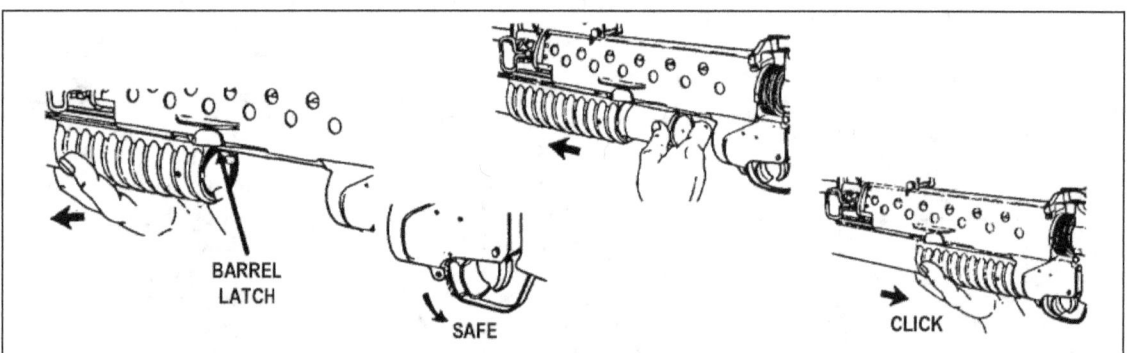

Figure 2-1. Loading the M203 grenade launcher.

WARNING

Keep the muzzle pointed downrange and clear of all soldiers.

Use the correct ammunition: never use high-velocity 40-mm ammunition designated for other 40-mm weapons such as the MK 19. High-velocity rounds are longer than those used in the M203 and may cause this weapon to explode.

2-3. UNLOADING

To unload the grenade launcher, the grenadier must first depress the barrel latch and move the barrel forward. The cartridge case or round should automatically eject. If the case is stuck, he taps it with a cleaning rod to remove it (Figure 2-2). He places the weapon on SAFE, then slides the barrel rearward, locking it to the breech.

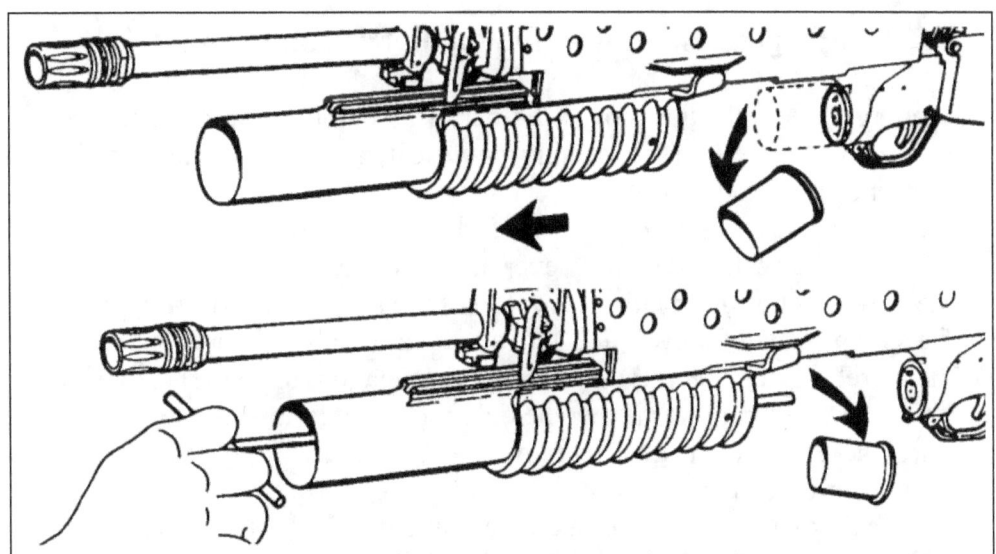

Figure 2-2. Unloading the M203 grenade launcher.

WARNING

If you are unloading a weapon that has not been fired, avoid detonation either by catching the ejected round or by holding the weapon close to the ground to reduce the distance the round can fall.

2-4. CYCLE OF FUNCTIONING

Knowing the M203's cycle of functioning from loading to firing helps grenadiers recognize and correct stoppages. Many of the actions described in this chapter occur at once, but here they are explained separately.

a. **Unlocking**. The cycle begins when the grenadier depresses the barrel latch to unlock the barrel assembly and slides the barrel assembly forward (Figure 2-3).

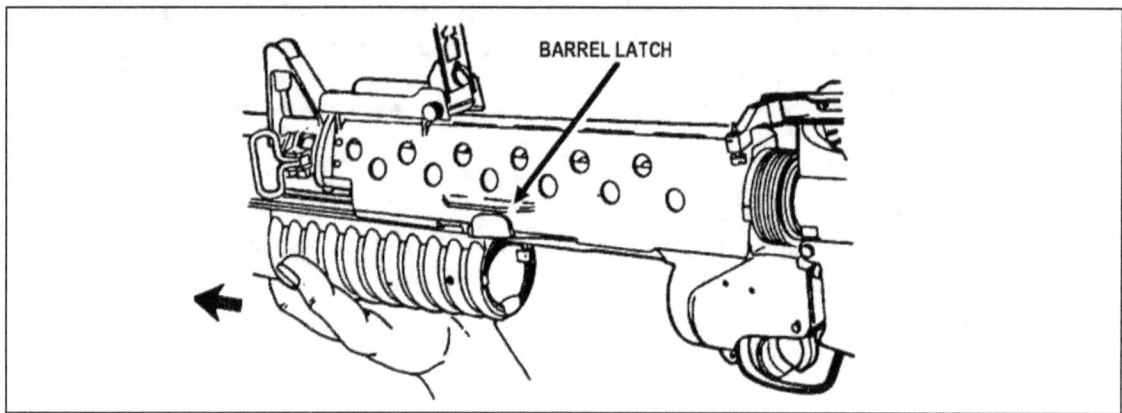

Figure 2-3. Unlocking the barrel assembly.

b. **Cocking**. The grenadier moves the barrel assembly forward, then backward, to cock the weapon. As the barrel assembly moves, it takes with it the barrel extension. Their movement causes the following to occur:

(1) The cocking lever is forced down as the barrel assembly and barrel extension, which are interlocked with the cocking lever, move forward.

(2) The movement of the cocking lever forces the spring-loaded firing pin to the rear.

(3) The spring-loaded follower also moves forward with the barrel extension.

(4) The barrel assembly continues forward, disengaging the barrel extension from the cocking lever. The cocking lever is then held down by the follower.

(5) When the grenadier begins to move the barrel assembly back to the rear, this forces the follower to the rear.

(6) The cocking lever again engages the barrel extension, which causes the firing pin to move slightly forward and engage the primary trigger sear. This cocks the weapon (Figure 2-4, page 2-4).

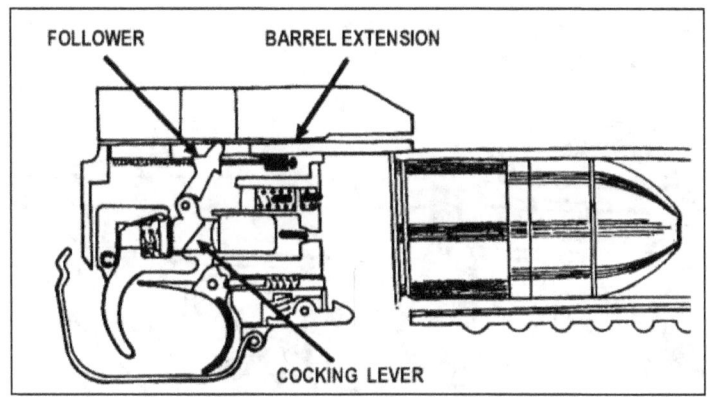

Figure 2-4. Cocking the M203 grenade launcher.

c. **Extracting**. Extracting and cocking occur at the same time. As the grenadier opens the barrel assembly, a spring-loaded extractor keeps the live round or spent cartridge case seated against the receiver until the barrel clears the cartridge case (Figure 2-5).

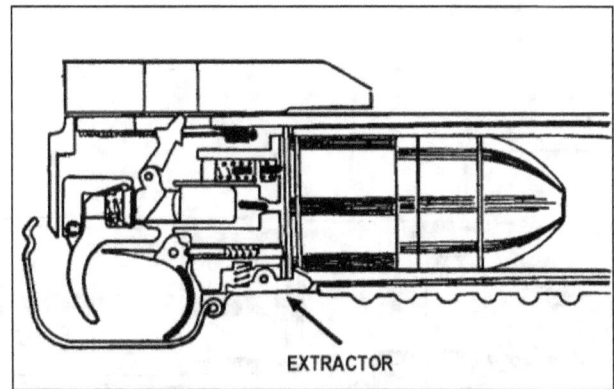

Figure 2-5. Extracting the round or cartridge case.

d. **Ejecting**. The spring-loaded ejector pushes the live round or spent cartridge case from the barrel assembly (Figure 2-6).

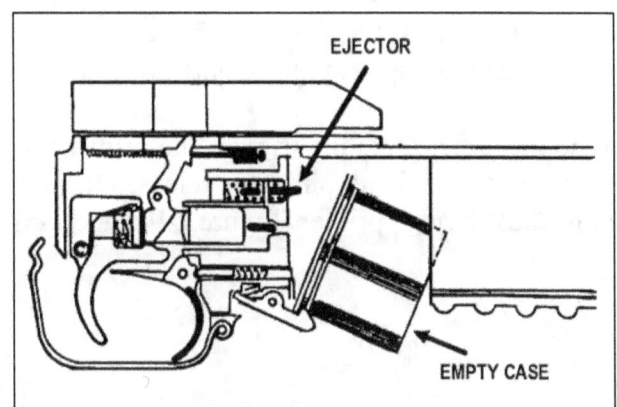

Figure 2-6. Ejecting the round or cartridge case.

e. **Loading**. With the barrel assembly open, the grenadier inserts a round into the breech end of the barrel (Figure 2-7).

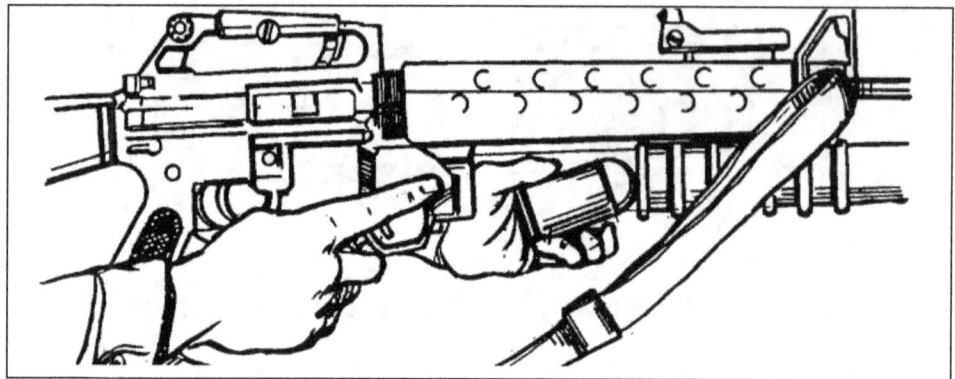

Figure 2-7. Loading the M203 grenade launcher.

f. **Chambering**. As the grenadier closes the breech end of the barrel assembly, the extractor contacts the rim of the cartridge and seats (chambers) the round firmly (Figure 2-8).

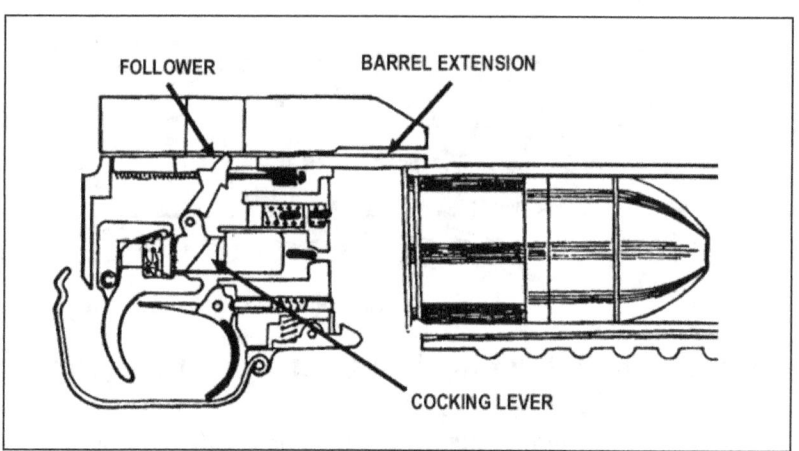

Figure 2-8. Chambering a round.

g. **Locking**. As the barrel assembly closes, the barrel latch engages it. The cocking lever engages the barrel extension so that it cannot move forward along the receiver assembly.

h. **Firing**. When the grenadier pulls the trigger, the primary trigger sear disengages from the bottom sear surface of the firing pin. This releases the spring-driven firing pin, forcing it forward against the cartridge primer (Figure 2-9, page 2-6).

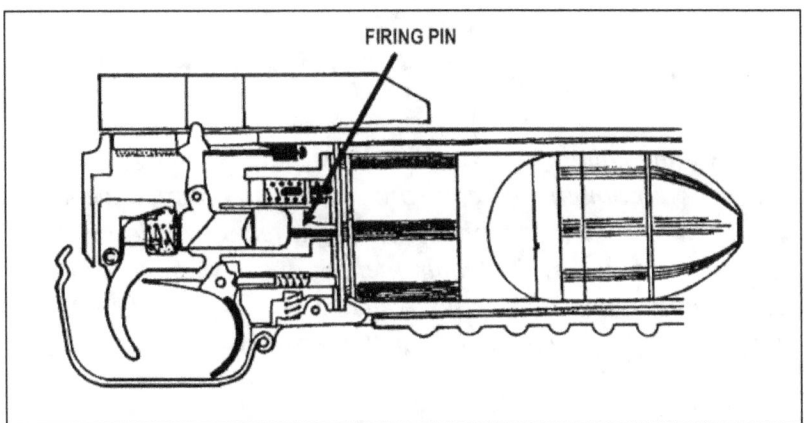

FIRING PIN

Figure 2-9. Firing the M203 grenade launcher.

CHAPTER 3
DESCRIPTION AND MAINTENANCE

Proper weapon maintenance is a vital part of all gunnery training programs. Good maintenance contributes to weapon effectiveness as well as to unit readiness. This chapter provides a technical description of the M203 grenade launcher, its components, and its ammunition. It also discusses proper procedures for clearing, disassembling, cleaning, lubricating, inspecting, and caring for the weapon.

3-1. DESCRIPTION

The M203 grenade launcher is a lightweight, single-shot, breech-loaded, pump action (sliding barrel), shoulder-fired weapon that is attached to an M16 rifle series (Figure 3-1), or the M4 carbine series with the M203A1 (Figure 3-2), and M4 carbine series with the rail system (Figure 3-3, page 3-2).

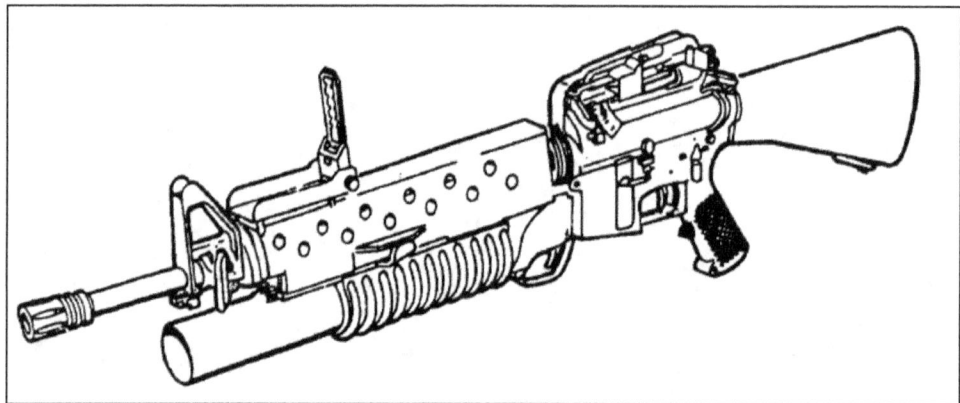

Figure 3-1. M203 grenade launcher (left side view).

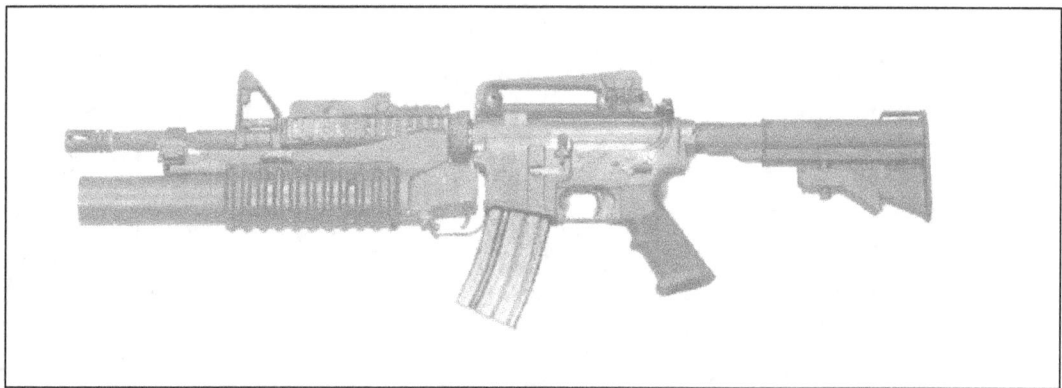

Figure 3-2. M4 carbine with M203A1 (left side view).

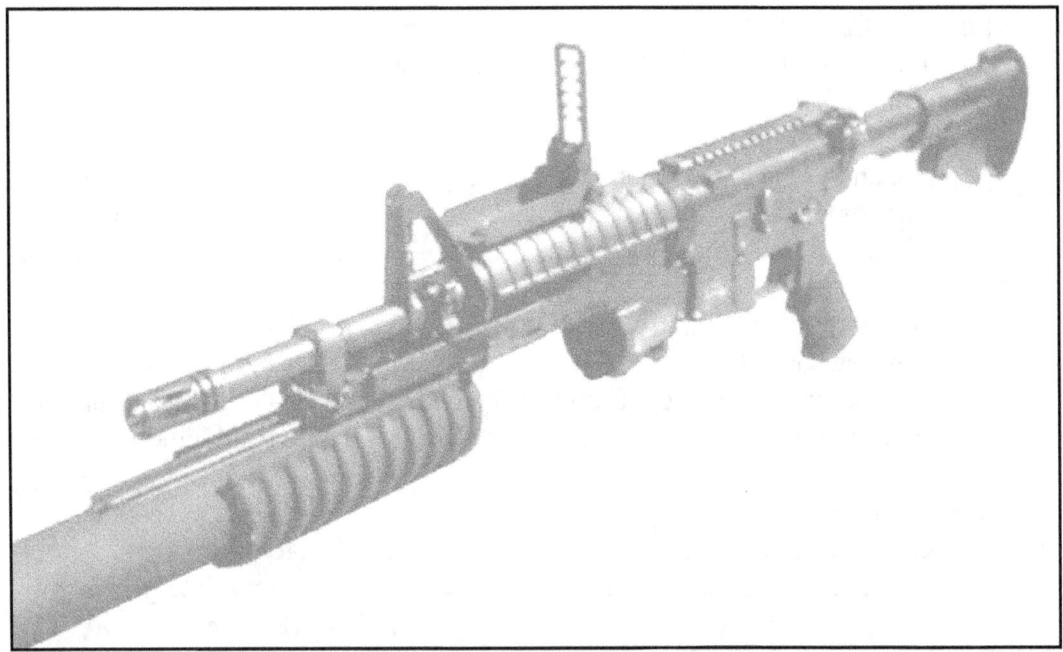

Figure 3-3. M4 carbine with rail system.

NOTES: 1. The M203 grenade launcher must be mounted to the M16 rifle series by the unit's armorer, and the M203A1 must be mounted to the M4 carbine rifle series by the unit's supporting DS maintenance company IAW instructions contained in TM 9-1010221-23&P.

2. Individual soldiers should not attempt to either mount or dismount the grenade launcher to the weapon.

3-2. TECHNICAL DATA

The technical data for the M203/M203A1 grenade launcher is as follows:

a. **Weapon**.

Length:

    Rifle and grenade launcher (overall) ....99.0 cm (39 inches)

    Barrel only ....30.5 cm (12 inches)

    Rifling ....25.4 cm (10 inches)

Weight:

    Launcher, unloaded...1.4 kg (3.0 pounds)

    Launcher, loaded..1.6 kg (3.5 pounds)

    Rifle and grenade launcher, both fully loaded...........5.0 kg (11.0 pounds)

Number of lands...6 right hand twist

b. **Ammunition**.

Caliber...40 mm

Weight..About 227 grams
(8 ounces)

c. **Operational Characteristics**.

Action...Single shot

Sights:

    Front...Leaf sight assembly

    Rear ....Quadrant sight

Chamber pressure...206,325 kilopascals
(35,000 psi)

Muzzle velocity..76 mps (250 fps)

Maximum range ....About 400 meters
(1,312 feet)

Maximum effective range:

    Fire-team sized area target..350 meters (1,148 feet)

    Vehicle or weapon point target..................................150 meters (492 feet)

Minimum safe firing range (HE):

    Training...130 meters (426 feet)

    Combat...31 meters (102 feet)

Minimum arming range ....About 14 to 38 meters
(46 to 125 feet)

Rate of fire ....5 to 7 rounds per minute

Minimum combat load..36 HE rounds

WARNING

When firing close-in, such as in urban areas, trenches, and other restrictive terrain, observe the minimum arming range to ensure the round clears other friendly forces.

3-3. COMPONENTS

Figure 3-4 shows the M203's major components, and the following paragraphs describe their purposes. The sight assemblies, the trigger and trigger guard, and the safety are shown in Figures 3-5 through 3-10.

a. **Handguard**. The handguard assembly houses the rifle barrel (Figure 3-4).

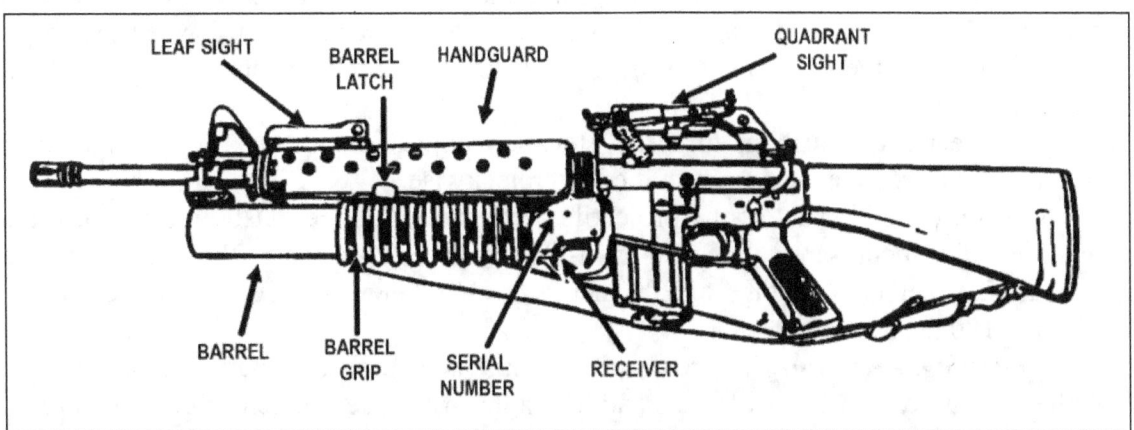

Figure 3-4. Components of the M203 grenade launcher.

b. **Quadrant Sight Assembly**. The quadrant sight assembly, which attaches to the left side of the rifle's carrying handle, enables the grenadier to adjust for elevation and windage (Figure 3-4). This assembly consists of the sight, mounting screw, sight latch, rear sight aperture, sight aperture arm, front sight post, and sight post arm (Figure 3-5).

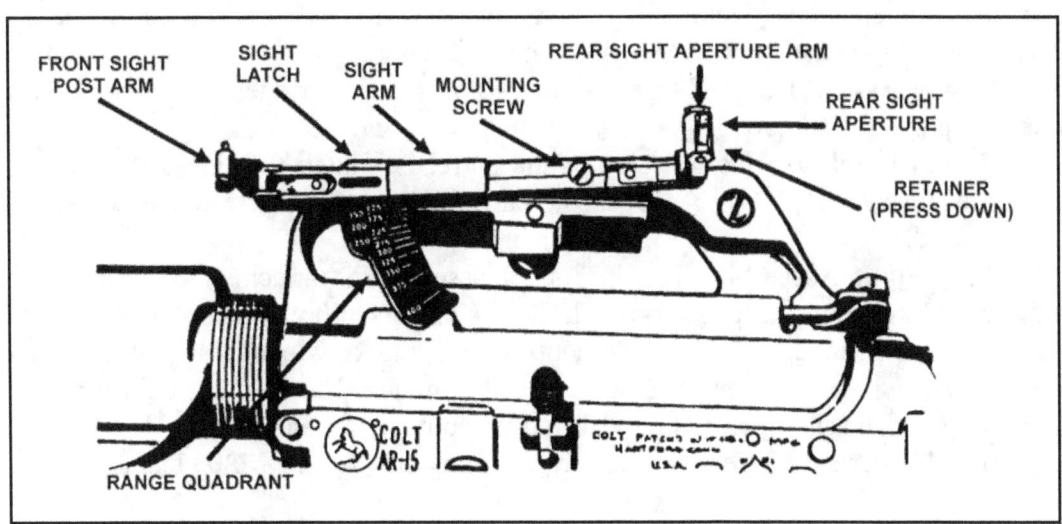

Figure 3-5. Quadrant sight assembly.

(1) *Clamp, Bracket Assembly, and Mounting Screw*. The clamp and the bracket assembly hold the quadrant sight on the rifle's carrying handle. The mounting screw inserts through the right side of the clamp and into the bracket assembly.

(2) *Sight Arm and Range Quadrant*. The sight arm mounts both the sight aperture arm (which holds the rear sight aperture) and the sight post arm (which holds the front

sight post). This procedure allows the sight to pivot on the range quadrant to the desired range setting. The range quadrant is graduated in 25-meter increments from 50 to 400 meters. Applying rearward pressure on the sight latch releases the quadrant sight arm so it can move along the range quadrant. Centering the number in the rear sight aperture selects the desired range. Releasing the sight latch locks the sight in position.

(3) *Front Sight Post*. The front sight post mounts on the sight post arm by means of a pivot bracket. To prevent damage to the sights, keep the bracket closed when the sights are not in use. Use the sight post as follows to make minor adjustments in elevation when zeroing the launcher:

(a) To decrease elevation, turn the elevation adjustment screw on the sight post clockwise; to increase elevation, turn it counterclockwise.

(b) To move the impact of the projectile 5 meters at a range of 200 meters, turn the elevation adjustment screw one full turn--360 degrees. To move the impact of the projectile 2.5 meters at a range of 200 meters, turn the elevation adjustment screw one half turn--180 degrees.

(4) *Rear Sight Aperture*. The rear sight aperture is on the sight aperture arm, which is attached to the rear portion of the quadrant sight arm. Use the rear sight aperture as follows to make minor adjustments in deflection (windage) when zeroing the launcher:

(a) To move the impact to the left, press the rear sight aperture retainer down and move the rear sight aperture away from the barrel; to move to the right, move it toward the barrel.

(b) To move the impact of the projectile 1.5 meters at a range of 200 meters, move the rear sight aperture one notch.

c. **Receiver Assembly and Serial Number**. The receiver assembly houses the firing mechanism and ejection system and supports the barrel assembly. On the left side of the receiver assembly is the launcher's serial number (Figure 3-4).

d. **Barrel Assembly**. The barrel assembly holds the cartridges ready for firing and directs the projectile (Figure 3-4).

e. **Barrel Latch**. On the left side of the barrel is a latch that locks the barrel and receiver together (Figure 3-4). To open the barrel, depress the barrel latch and slide the barrel forward.

f. **Leaf Sight Assembly**. The leaf sight assembly is attached to the top of the handguard (Figure 3-6, on page 3-6). The leaf sight assembly consists of the sight, its base and mount, an elevation adjustment screw, and a windage adjustment screw. Elevation and windage scales are marked on the mount. The folding, adjustable, open ladder design of the sight permits rapid firing without sight manipulation. The front sight post of the M16-series rifle serves as the front aiming post for the M203 leaf sight.

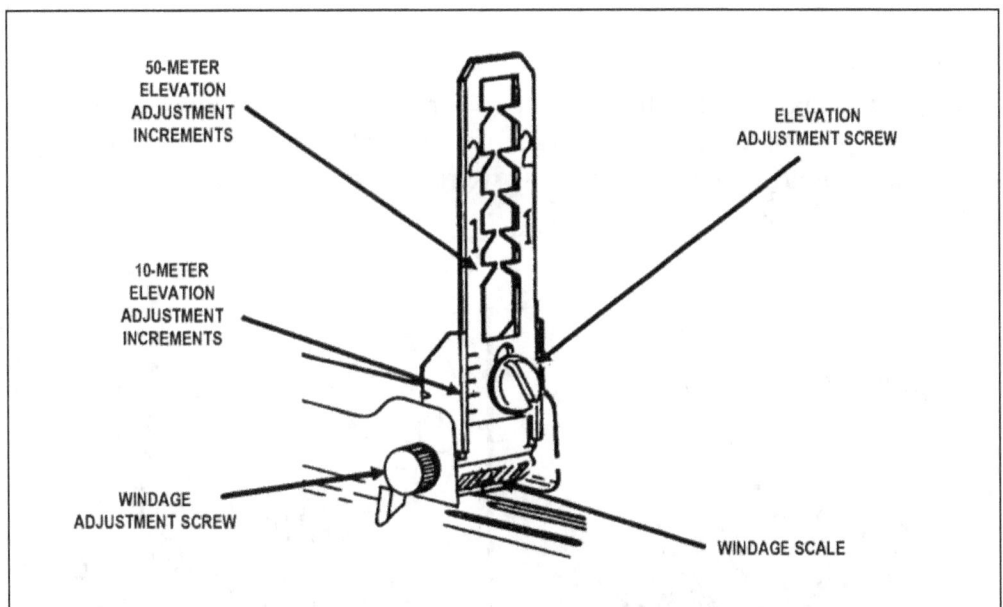

Figure 3-6. Leaf sight assembly.

(1) ***Sight Base***. Two mounting screws permanently attach the sight base to the rifle handguard. When the sight is down or not in use, the base protects it from damage.

(2) ***Sight Mount and Sight***. The grenadier uses the sight mount, which is attached to the sight base, to raise or lower the sight. Though the range is not marked on the sight in meters, the sight is graduated in 50-meter increments from 50 to 250 meters, which are marked with a "1" at 100 meters and a "2" at 200 meters.

(3) ***Elevation Adjustment Screw and Elevation Scale***. The screw attaches the sight to its mount. When the screw is loosened, the sight can be moved up or down to make minor adjustments in elevation during the zeroing procedure. The rim of a 40-mm cartridge case is useful for turning the screw. Raising the sight increases the range; lowering the sight decreases the range. The elevation scale consists of five lines spaced equally on the sight. The index line is to the left of the sight. Moving the sight one increment moves the impact of the projectile 10 meters in elevation at a range of 200 meters.

(4) ***Windage Screw and Windage Scale***. The knob on the left end of the windage screw is used to make minor deflection adjustments during the zeroing procedure. The scale has a zero line in its center and two lines spaced equally on each side of the zero line. At a range of 200 meters, turning the knob on the windage scale one increment to the ***left*** moves the impact of the projectile 1.5 meters to the ***right***.

DANGER
THE 50-METER MARK ON THE LEAF SIGHT BLADE IS MARKED IN RED TO EMPHASIZE THAT THIS RANGE MUST NOT BE USED FOR ZEROING PROCEDURES. DUE TO FRAGMENTATION, ZEROING IS EXTREMELY DANGEROUS AT 50 METERS OR LESS.

---

f. **Trigger Guard**. The trigger guard protects the trigger (A, Figure 3-6). Depressing the rear portion of the trigger guard rotates it down and away from the magazine well of the rifle, which allows the weapon to be fired while the firer is wearing gloves or mittens (B, Figure 3-7).

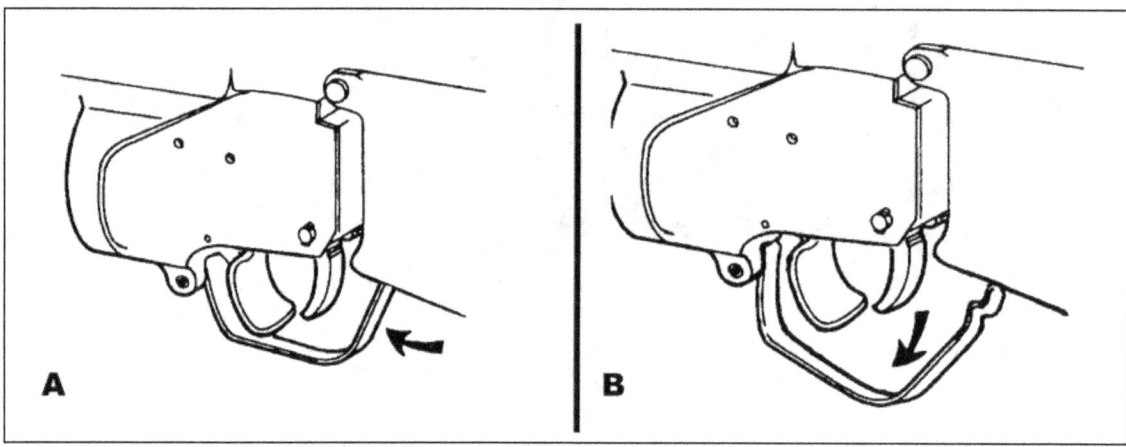

Figure 3-7. Trigger guard.

g. **Safety**. The safety is inside the trigger guard, just in front of the trigger. For the launcher to fire, the safety must be forward. When the safety is rearward, the launcher is on SAFE. The safety is manually adjusted (Figure 3-8).

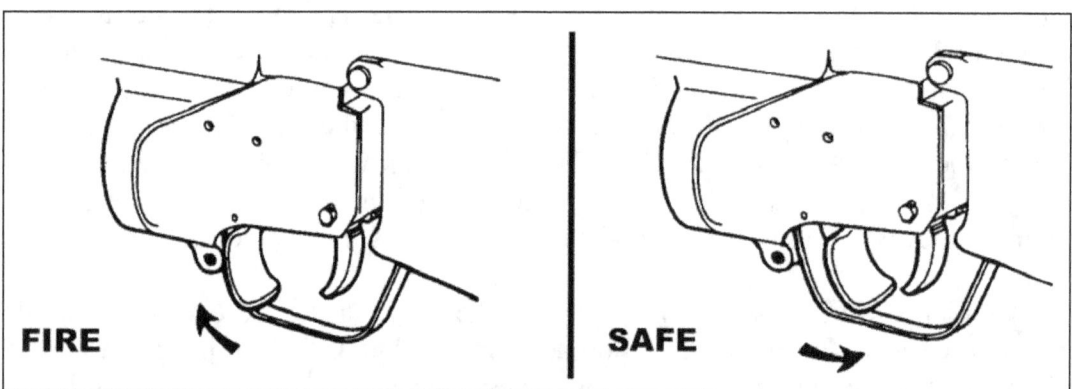

Figure 3-8. Safety.

3-4. AMMUNITION

The M203 grenade launcher uses several fixed-type, low-velocity 40-mm rounds. The M203 fires high-explosive, illuminating, signaling, CS, training, and multipurpose ammunition. **This paragraph discusses only the most commonly used ammunition.**

> **WARNING**
>
> If fired into snow or mud, 40-mm rounds may not hit hard enough to detonate. An undetonated round may explode when stepped on or driven over. During training in snow or mud, avoid this hazard by firing only TP rounds.

a. **Types, Characteristics, and Capabilities**. All M203 grenade launcher rounds are fixed rounds (Figure 3-9). (TM 43-0001-28 provides more details.)

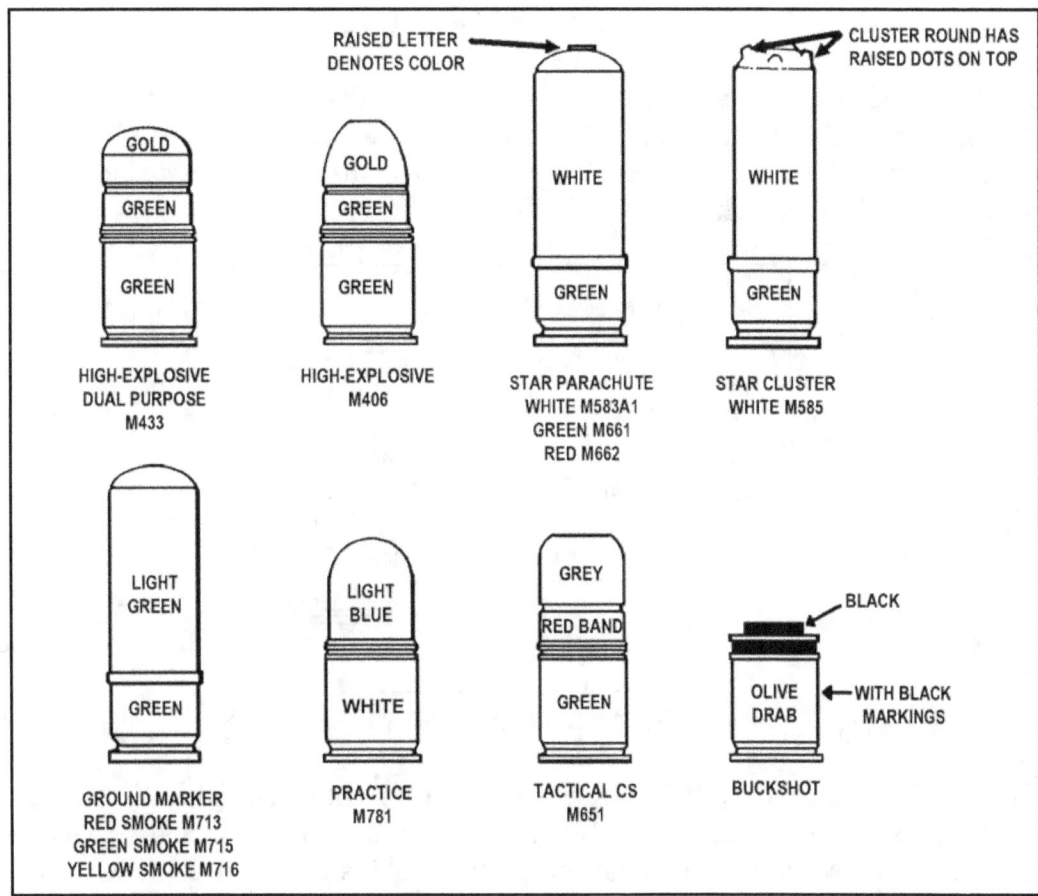

Figure 3-9. Cartridges for the M203 grenade launcher.

(1) *High-Explosive Dual Purpose Round*. The HEDP round has an olive drab aluminum skirt with a steel cup attached, white markings, and a gold ogive (head of the round) (Figure 3-10). It penetrates at least 5 cm (2 inches) when fired straight at steel armor at 150 meters or less, or, at a point target it arms between 14 and 27 meters, causes casualties within a 130-meter radius, and has a kill radius of 5 meters.

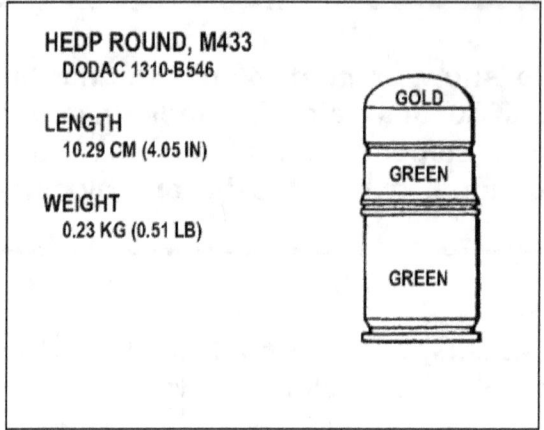

Figure 3-10. HEDP round.

(2) ***High-Explosive Round.*** The HE round has an olive drab aluminum skirt with a steel projectile attached, gold markings, and a yellow ogive (Figure 3-11). It arms between 14 and 27 meters, produces a ground burst that causes casualties within a 130-meter radius, and has a kill radius of 5 meters.

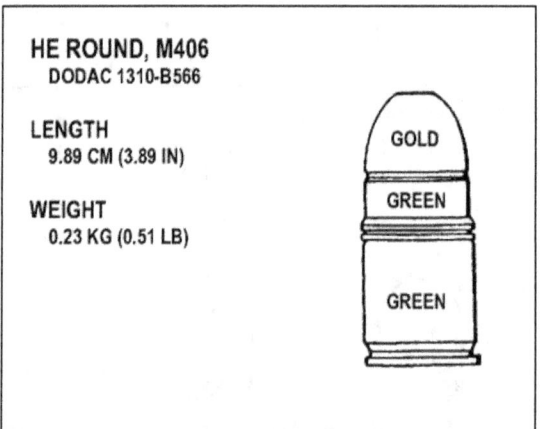

Figure 3-11. HE round.

(3) ***Star Parachute Round.*** This round is white impact or bar alloy aluminum with black markings (Figure 3-12, page 3-10). It is used for illumination and signals and is lighter and more accurate than comparable handheld signal rounds. The parachute attached to the round deploys upon ejection to lower the candle at 7 feet per second. The candle burns for about 40 seconds. A raised letter on the top of the round denotes the color of the parachute.

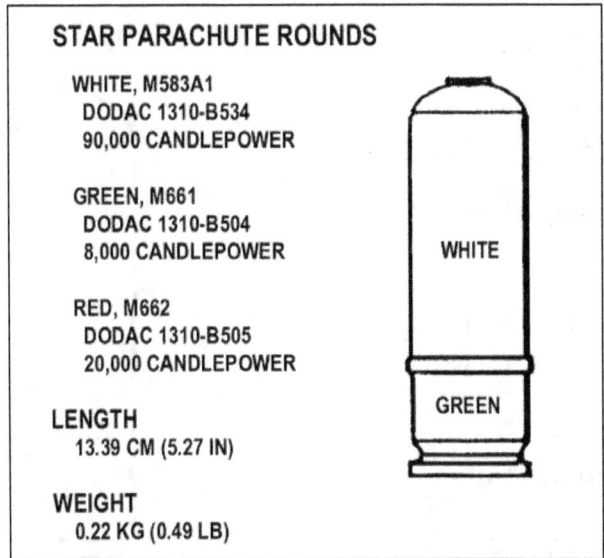

Figure 3-12. Star parachute round.

(4) *White Star Cluster Round*. This round is white impact or bar aluminum alloy with black markings (Figure 3-13). The attached plastic ogive has five raised dots for night identification. The round is used for illumination or signals. It is lighter and more accurate than comparable handheld signal rounds. The individual stars burn for about 7 seconds during free fall.

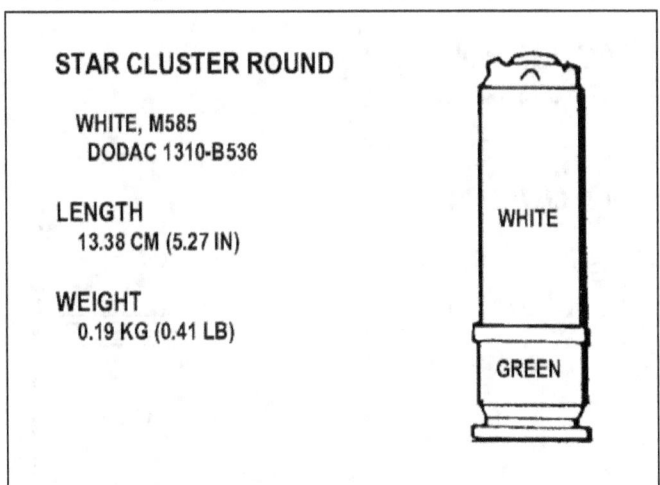

Figure 3-13. White star cluster round.

(5) *Ground Marker Round*. This round is light green impact aluminum with black markings (Figure 3-14). It is used for aerial identification and for marking the location of soldiers on the ground. It arms between 15 and 45 meters. If a fuze fails to function on impact, the output mixture provided in the front end of the delay casing backs up the impact feature. The color of the ogive indicates the color of the smoke.

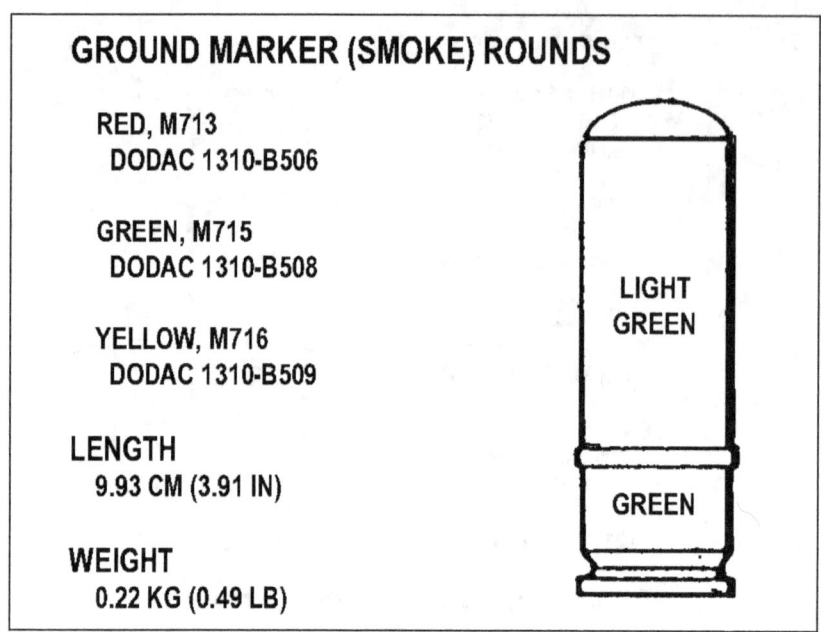

GROUND MARKER (SMOKE) ROUNDS

RED, M713
DODAC 1310-B506

GREEN, M715
DODAC 1310-B508

YELLOW, M716
DODAC 1310-B509

LENGTH
9.93 CM (3.91 IN)

WEIGHT
0.22 KG (0.49 LB)

LIGHT GREEN

GREEN

Figure 3-14. Ground marker round (smoke).

(6) *Practice Round*. Used for practice, this round is blue zinc or aluminum with white markings (Figure 3-15). It produces a yellow or orange signature on impact, arms between 14 and 27 meters, and has a danger radius of 20 meters.

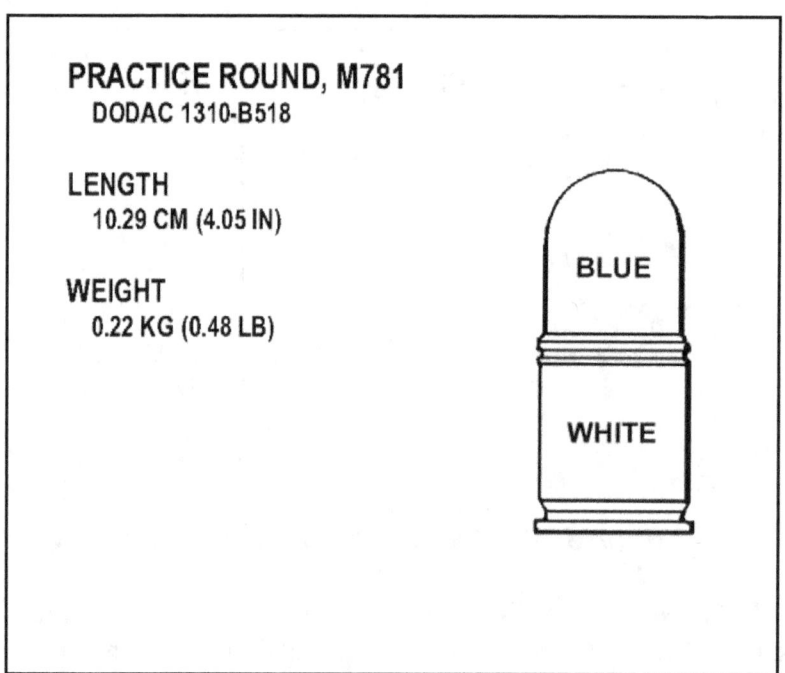

PRACTICE ROUND, M781
DODAC 1310-B518

LENGTH
10.29 CM (4.05 IN)

WEIGHT
0.22 KG (0.48 LB)

BLUE

WHITE

Figure 3-15. Practice round.

(7) *CS Round*. This round is gray aluminum with a green casing and black markings (Figure 3-16). Though it is a multipurpose round, it is most effective for riot control and

in MOUT. It arms between 10 and 30 meters and produces a white cloud of CS gas on impact.

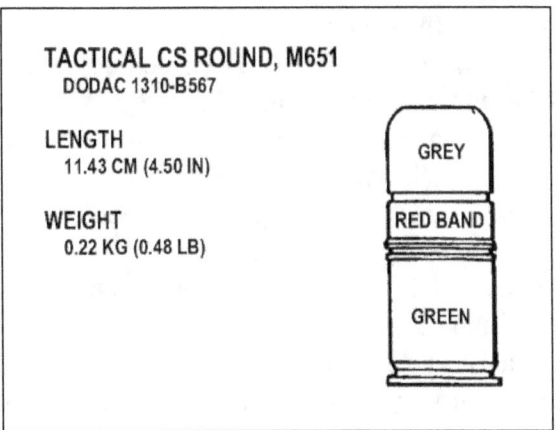

Figure 3-16. CS round.

(8) ***Buckshot Round***. This round is olive drab with black markings (Figure 3-17). Though it is a multipurpose round, it is most effective in thick vegetated areas or for room clearing. Inside it has at least 2,000 pellets, which cast a cone of fire 30 meters wide and 30 meters high and travel at 269 meters per second. Be sure to aim buckshot rounds at the foot of the target. The round has no mechanical-type fuse.

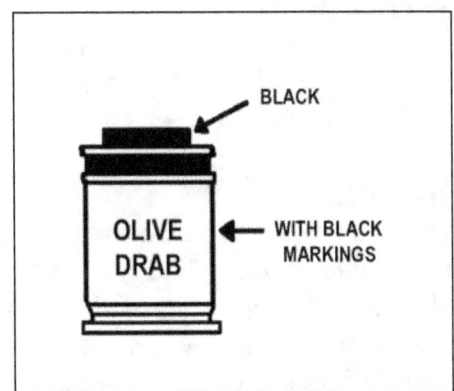

Figure 3-17. Buckshot round.

b.   **Storage**. Ammunition should be stored under cover. If this is not possible, store it at least 15 centimeters (6 inches) above the ground and covered with a double layer of tarpaulins. Place the tarpaulins so they protect the ammunition but still allow for ventilation. Dig trenches to prevent water from flowing under the ammunition.

c.   **Care, Handling, and Preservation**. Do not open ammunition containers until you are ready to use the ammunition. Ammunition removed from the airtight container is likely to corrode, particularly in damp climates. Soldiers must take the following precautions:

(1) ***Protect Ammunition from Mud, Dirt, and Water***. If it gets wet or dirty, wipe it off before using it. Also, wipe off lightly corroded cartridges as soon as the corrosion is

discovered. Do not fire heavily corroded or dented projectiles or those with loose parts or particles.

(2) *Avoid Exposing Ammunition to the Direct Rays of the Sun.* Hot powder can cause excessive pressure when the round is fired.

(3) *Do Not Lubricate Ammunition.* This can cause dust and other abrasives to collect on it and damage the operating parts of the launcher.

d. **Packaging.** Ammunition packaging varies according to the type of ammunition:

(1) *HE, HEDP, and TP.* Each box of HE, HEDP, and TP ammunition contains 1 can with 6 bandoleers of 12 rounds each, for a total of 72 rounds.

(2) *Smoke and Cluster Ammunition.* Each wire-bound box of smoke and cluster ammunition contains 2 cans with 22 rounds each, for a total of 44 rounds.

(3) *CS Ammunition.* Each box of CS ammunition contains 2 cans with 4 bandoleers of 6 rounds each, for a total of 48 rounds.

(4) *Buckshot.* Each box of buckshot ammunition contains 12 bandoleers of 6 rounds each, for a total of 72 rounds.

3-5. CLEARING PROCEDURES

The soldier must clear the weapon before performing maintenance on it. FM 23-9 (3.22.9) provides instructions for clearing an M16-series rifle. To clear the grenade launcher--

a. Push in the release button and pull the barrel forward.
b. Watch to see if a round extracts.
c. Place the safety on SAFE.
d. Inspect the breech to ensure a round is not present.
e. Pull the barrel to the rear until it clicks. This cocks the weapon.
f. Place the safety on FIRE.

3-6. GENERAL DISASSEMBLY

When disassembling the weapon, the soldier places each part, as it is removed, on a clean, flat surface such as a table, shelter half, or disassembly mat. This aids in reassembly and simplifies the task of keeping up with the parts. The soldier will later assemble the grenade launcher in the reverse order that he disassembled it (paragraph 3-9). (Only ordnance personnel disassemble the grenade launcher beyond the steps described here.) To disassemble the weapon--

a. Loosen the mounting screw and remove the quadrant sight assembly from the carrying handle of the M16-series rifle (Figure 3-18, page 3-14).

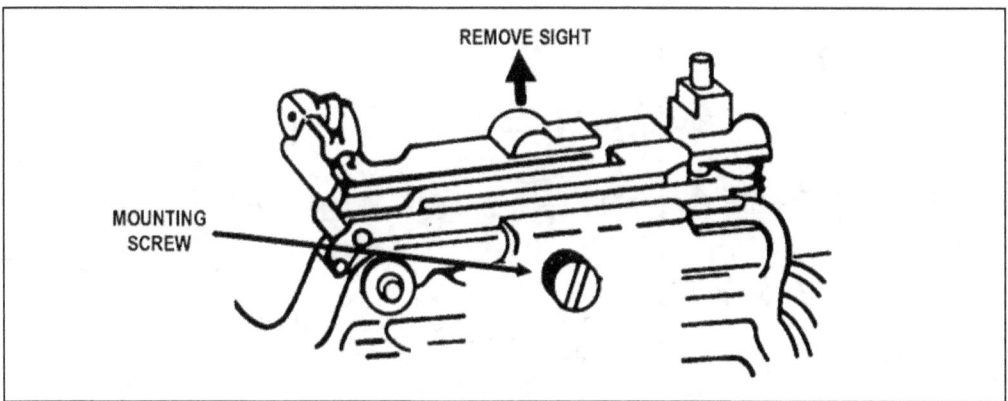

Figure 3-18. Removing the quadrant sight assembly.

b.   Remove the barrel assembly and handguard assembly, in either order:

(1) ***Barrel Assembly First.*** Push the barrel latch and move the barrel forward until it hits the barrel stop. On the left side of the handguard, insert a cleaning rod into the fourth hole back from the muzzle, depress the barrel stop, and slide the barrel forward and off (Figure 3-19).

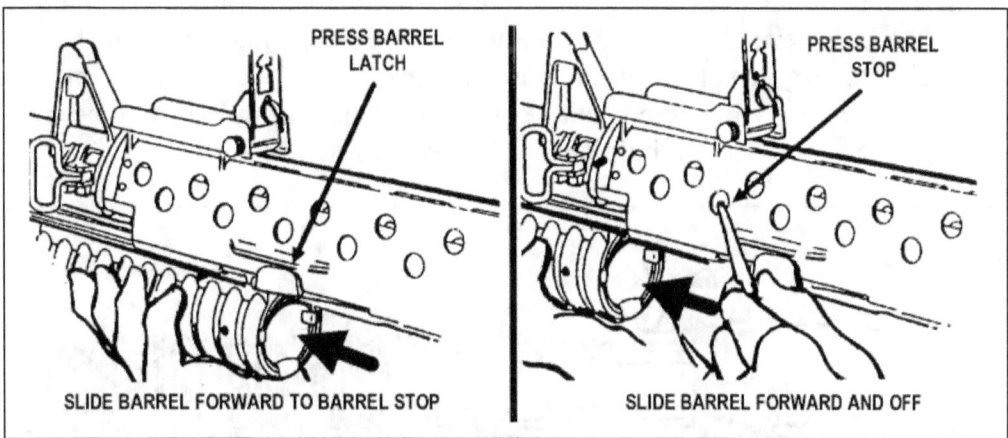

Figure 3-19. Removing the barrel assembly
before the handguard assembly.

(2) ***Handguard Assembly First.*** Pull back on the M16's slip ring and remove the handguard by pulling it up and back. Push the barrel latch and move the barrel forward until it hits the barrel stop. Use a cleaning rod to depress the barrel stop and slide the barrel forward and off (Figure 3-20).

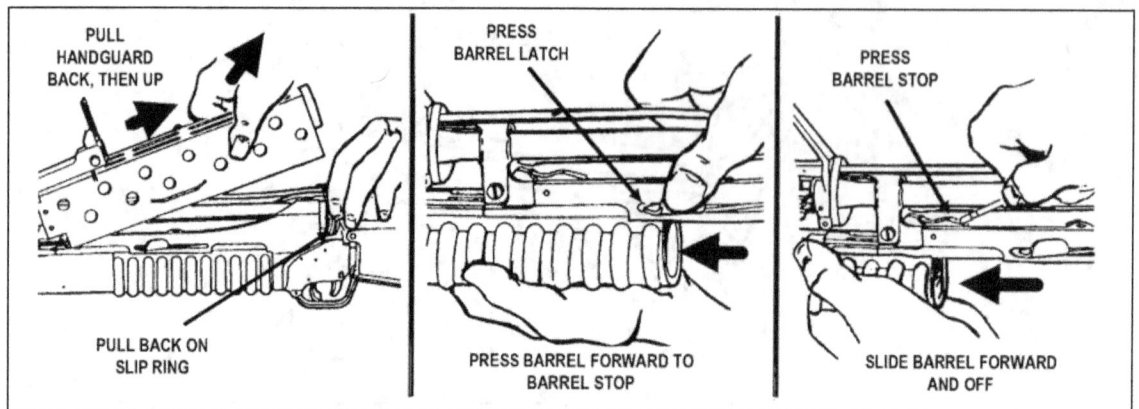

**Figure 3-20. Removing the handguard assembly
before the barrel assembly.**

3-7. CLEANING AND LUBRICATION

After firing the grenade launcher, or if it has been idle for a long time, the soldier must clean and lubricate it as follows:

a. **Bore**. Attach a clean, dry rag to the thong and thoroughly moisten the rag with CLP. Pull the rag through the bore several times. Attach the bore brush to the thong, pull it through the bore several times, and follow this with more rags moistened with CLP (Figure 3-21). Pull dry rags through the bore, and inspect each rag as it is removed. The bore is clean when a dry rag comes out clean. Finally, pull a rag lightly moistened with CLP through the bore to leave a light coat of lubricant inside the barrel.

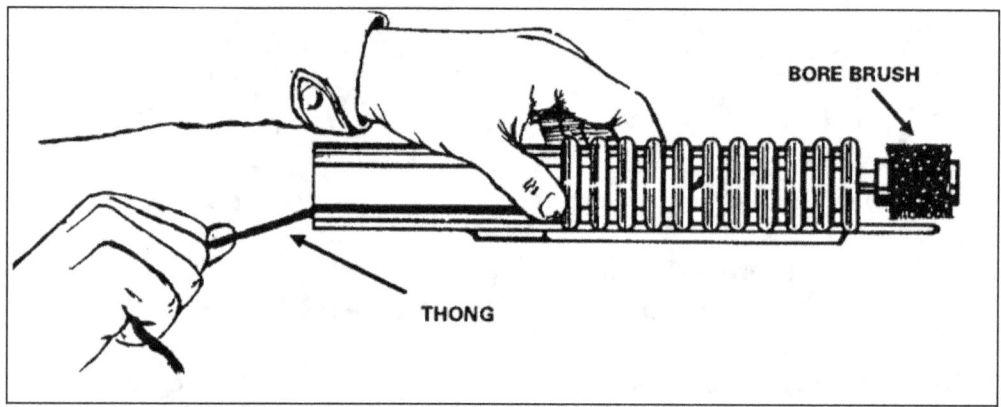

Figure 3-21. Cleaning the barrel with thong and bore brush.

b. **Breech Insert**. Clean the face of the breech insert with a patch and CLP. Remove this CLP with dry rags; then lubricate the breech with a new, light coat of CLP.

c. **Other Parts**. Use a brush and dry rags to clean all the other parts and surfaces. After cleaning, apply a light coat of CLP to the outside of the launcher.

d. **Safety Mechanism**. Clean the safety mechanism properly with CLP; then lubricate it with CLP.

e. **Special Lubrication Requirements**. Lubricate the grenade launcher only with CLP and IAW the following environmental guidelines:

(1) *Extreme Heat*. Lubricate with CLP, grade 2.

(2) *Damp or Salty Air*. Clean the weapon and apply CLP, grade 2, frequently.

(3) *Sandy or Dusty Air*. Clean the weapon and apply CLP, grade 2, frequently. Remove excess CLP with a rag after each application.

(4) *Temperatures Below Freezing*. When the weapon is brought in from a cold area to a warm area, keep it wrapped in a parka or blanket, and allow it to reach room temperature gradually. If condensation forms on the weapon, dry and lubricate it at room temperature with CLP, grade 2, before returning it to cold weather. Otherwise, ice will form inside the mechanism.

NOTE: Although CLP provides the required lubrication at temperatures down to -35°F (-37°C), it will not flow from a 1/2-ounce bottle at temperatures below 0°F (-17°C).

3-8.   INSPECTION

Inspection begins with the weapon already disassembled into its major groups or assemblies. Parts with shiny surfaces are serviceable. The following parts of the weapon and related equipment are inspected IAW TM 9-1010-221-10:

a.   **All Parts**. Check for wear and damage, including burrs, scratches, and nicks.

b.   **Handguard**. Check for cracks, dents, or distortion that prevents its firm attachment to the rifle.

c.   **Leaf Sight Assembly**. Check for bent or damaged parts, rust or corrosion, and illegibility of markings.

d.   **Barrel**. Check for cracks or dents.

e.   **Cartridge and Retainers**. Check for breakage, bends, chips, or missing parts.

NOTE: Take any unserviceable part to the armorer, who will determine its serviceability and replace parts as necessary.

3-9.   GENERAL ASSEMBLY

The soldier assembles the grenade launcher in the reverse order of disassembly.

a.   Install the barrel by pressing the barrel stop and sliding the barrel into the receiver (Figure 3-22).

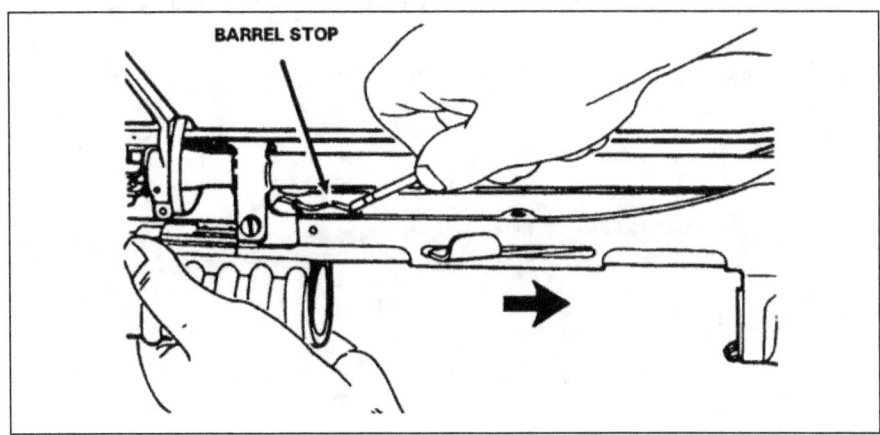

Figure 3-22. Installing the barrel.

b. Lock the barrel by moving it rearward until it closes with a click (Figure 3-23).

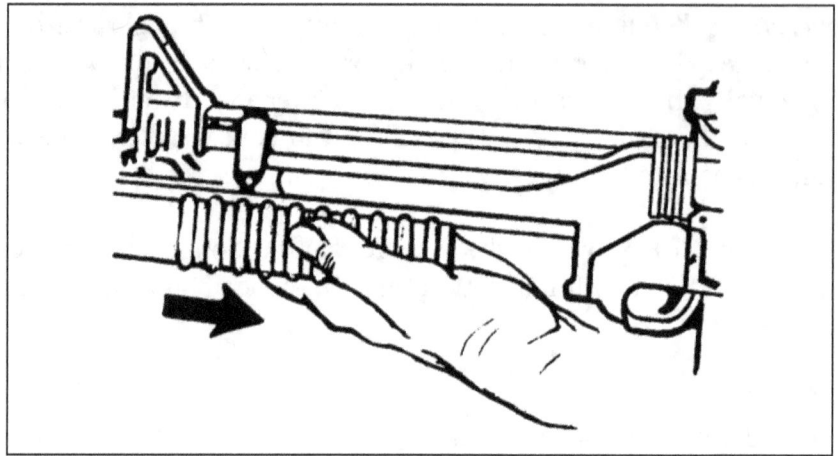

Figure 3-23. Locking the barrel.

c. Install the handguard and secure it with the slip ring (Figure 3-24).

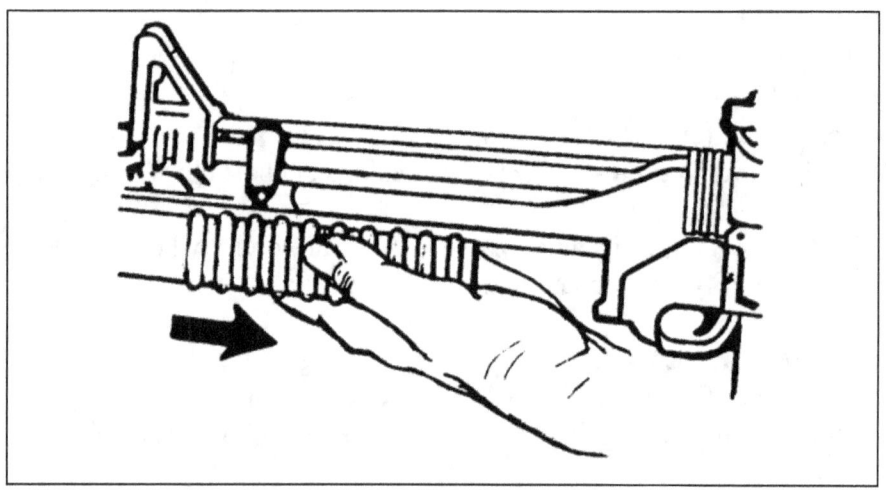

Figure 3-24. Installing and securing the handguard.

d. Install the quadrant sight assembly (Figure 3-25).

Figure 3-25. Installing the quadrant sight assembly.

e. Perform a function check to ensure that the grenade launcher has been assembled correctly. Notify the unit armorer at once if the launcher fails to function. Conduct the function check in this order:

(1) Check the proper operation of the sear. Cock the launcher and pull the trigger. The firing pin should release with a metallic click. Hold the trigger to the rear and cock the launcher again. Release the trigger, then pull. The firing pin should again release.

> **WARNING**
> If the sear malfunctions, the launcher could fire without the trigger being pulled.

---

(2) Check the safety by pulling the trigger in both the SAFE and FIRE positions. The launcher must be cocked before the safety can be placed in the SAFE position.

(3) Check the leaf sight assembly windage adjustment screw for proper operation. Move the elevation adjustment screw only if the weapon has been zeroed.

(4) Move the barrel forward and back to be sure the barrel stop and barrel latch function.

3-10. CARE AND HANDLING

Certain steps must be taken before, during, and after firing to properly maintain the grenade launcher.

a. **Before firing**.
- Wipe the bore dry.
- Inspect the weapon as outlined in the operator's technical manual.
- Ensure the weapon is properly lubricated.

b. **During firing**.
- Periodically inspect the weapon to ensure that it is lubricated.

- When malfunctions or stoppages occur, follow the procedures outlined in Chapter 4.

3-11.   CARE AND HANDLING UNDER NBC CONDITIONS

If contamination is anticipated, the soldier should apply CLP to all outer metal surfaces of the weapon. Ammunition, however, should never be lubricated. The soldier should keep the weapon covered as much as possible. If the weapon is contaminated, he should decontaminate it IAW FM 3-3 and FM 3-4 and then clean and lubricate it.

3-12.   DECONTAMINATION

Leaders must try to reduce the penetration of contaminants and exposure to them. Contaminated material is disposed of IAW SOP.

   a.   **Nuclear**. Wipe off the weapon with warm soapy water. Otherwise, use towelettes or rags. (FM 3-5 provides details.)

   b.   **Biological**. Use towelettes from the M258A1 kit to wipe off the weapon. If these are not available, wash with soap and water.

   c.   **Chemical**. Use soap and water or towelettes as for biological contamination.

CHAPTER 4
PERFORMANCE PROBLEMS AND DESTRUCTION

This chapter identifies some of the problems that can cause the M203 grenade launcher to perform incorrectly. It also explains how to identify unserviceable parts and how to destroy the weapon when authorized to do so.

4-1. MALFUNCTIONS

A malfunction occurs when a mechanical failure prevents the weapon from firing properly. Neither defective ammunition nor improper operation of the weapon by the firer is a malfunction. The weapon should be cleaned, lubricated, and retried. If it still fails to function, it should be turned in to the unit armorer. Table 4-1 shows probable causes and corrective action for each type of malfunction.

Malfunction	Probable Cause	Corrective Action
Failure to cock	Broken sear	Notify unit maintenance
	Improper assembly of cocking lever	
	Loose, broken, or missing cocking lever spring pin	
Failure to lock	Excess plastic on breech end of barrel assembly	

Table 4-1. Malfunctions.

4-2. STOPPAGES

A stoppage is an unintentional interruption in the cycle of operation or functioning that may be cleared by immediate action. A stoppage is classified by its relationship to the cycle of functioning. Table 4-2 on page 4-2 shows the types of stoppages.

Stoppage	Probable Cause	Corrective Action
Failure to fire	Safety on	Place in fire position
	Empty chamber	Load
	Faulty ammunition	Reload
	Water or excess lubricant in firing pin well	Hand cycle weapon several times, to include pulling the trigger
	Worn or broken firing pin	Notify unit maintenance
	Dirt or residue in firing pin recess	Clean
	Blurred sear or firing pin	Notify unit maintenance
	Dirty firing pin well opening	
	Weak or broken firing pin spring	
Failure to extract	Defective extractor on spring or spring pin	
	Ruptured cartridge case	Remove from barrel
Failure to eject	Worn, broken, or missing ejector spring or retainer	Notify unit maintenance
Failure to chamber	Faulty ammunition	Reload
	Dirty chamber	Clean bore and chamber
Safety fails to stay in position	Missing spring pin or broken or worn safety	Notify unit maintenance

Table 4-2. Stoppages.

4-3.   IMMEDIATE ACTION

Immediate action refers to anything a soldier does to reduce a stoppage without taking time to look for the cause. Immediate action should be taken in the event of either a hangfire or misfire. Either can be caused by an ammunition defect or by a faulty firing mechanism. Any failure to fire must be considered a hangfire until that possibility is eliminated.

- A hangfire is a delay in the functioning of the round's propelling charge explosive train at the time of firing. The length of this delay is unpredictable, but in most cases, it ranges between a split second and 30 seconds. Such a delay in the functioning of the round could result from the presence of excess oil or grease, grit, sand, frost, or ice.

- A misfire is a complete failure of the weapon to fire. A misfire in itself is not dangerous, but because it cannot be immediately distinguished from a hangfire, it must be considered to be a hangfire until proven otherwise.

Because a stoppage may be caused by a hangfire, the following precautions must be observed until the round has been removed from the weapon and the cause of the failure determined:

a. Keep the M203 pointed downrange or at the target and keep everyone clear of its muzzle. If the stoppage occurs during training, shout MISFIRE and clear the area of any soldiers not needed for the operation.

b. Wait 30 seconds from the time of the failure before opening the barrel assembly to perform the unloading procedure.

c. After removing the round from the receiver, determine whether the round or the firing mechanism is defective. Examine the primer to see if it is dented. If the primer is dented, separate the round from other ammunition until it can be disposed of properly. However, if the primer is not dented, the firing mechanism is at fault. Once the cause of the failure to fire has been corrected, the round may be reloaded and fired.

WARNING

If you are unloading a weapon that has not been fired, avoid detonation either by catching the ejected round or by holding the weapon close to the ground to reduce the distance the round can fall.

4-4. REMEDIAL ACTION
Remedial action is any action taken by the gunner to restore his weapon to operational condition. Take remedial action only if immediate action does not remedy the problem.

4-5. DESTRUCTION PROCEDURES
Destruction of any military weapon is authorized only as a last resort to prevent the enemy from capturing or using it. This paragraph discusses planning for destruction, priorities and methods of destruction, and degree of damage. In combat situations, the commander has the authority to destroy weapons, but he must report doing so through channels.

a. **Planning**. SOPs for all units should contain a plan for destroying equipment. Having such a plan ensures that the damage is effective enough to deny use of the equipment to the enemy. The plan must be flexible enough in its designation of time, equipment, and personnel to meet any situation.

b. **Priorities of Destruction**. When lack of time prevents them from completely destroying equipment, soldiers must destroy the same essential parts on all like equipment. The order in which the parts should be destroyed (priority of destruction) is as follows:

(1) Bolt assembly (M16) and breech mechanism (M203).
(2) Barrels (both M16 and M203).
(3) Sights or sighting equipment (including nightsight).
(4) Optics mount.

c. **Methods of Destruction**. Equipment may be destroyed by any of several methods. The commander must use his imagination and resourcefulness to select the best method of destruction based on the facilities available. Time is usually critical. The methods of destruction are as follows:

(1) *Mechanical*. Use an axe, pick, sledgehammer, crowbar, or other heavy implement.

(2) *Burning*. Use gasoline, oil, incendiary grenades, other flammables, or a welding or cutting torch.

(3) *Demolition*. Use suitable explosives or ammunition or, as a last resort, hand grenades.

(4) *Disposal*. Bury essential parts, dump them in streams, or scatter them so widely that recovering them would be impossible.

d. **Degree of Damage**. The method of destruction used must damage equipment and essential spare parts to the extent that they cannot be restored to usable condition in the combat zone, either by repair or by cannibalization.

CHAPTER 5
MARKSMANSHIP TRAINING

Marksmanship training is conducted in three phases. This chapter discusses the first two phases: preliminary marksmanship training, which develops nonfiring individual skill proficiency (Section I), and basic gunnery, during which the soldier learns to apply the fundamentals of gunnery and to zero the M203 during qualification exercises in day, NBC, and night conditions (Section II). Chapter 6 discusses the third phase, advanced gunnery. Every phase has the same three objectives: to teach each grenadier to hit the target accurately with the first round, to adjust fire, and to do both quickly.

WARNING
Before allowing anyone to move between stations, ensure that all rifles and grenade launchers have been cleared, that bolts are to the rear, and that barrel assemblies are in the open position. Anyone observing an unsafe act should call CEASE FIRE and notify range personnel immediately.

Section I. PRELIMINARY MARKSMANSHIP TRAINING

Grenadiers and leaders must master marksmanship fundamentals before firing individually or collectively. During preliminary marksmanship training, grenadiers learn and demonstrate the individual skills that prepare them to fire live ammunition. After learning the characteristics and mechanics of the weapon (Chapters 2, 3, and 4), they learn the four fundamentals of marksmanship, sight manipulation, and response to fire commands. Dry-fire exercises are excellent for training to proficiency. Good preliminary marksmanship instruction improves individual proficiency, which in turn improves the proficiency of collective fire.

5-1. FOUR FUNDAMENTALS OF MARKSMANSHIP

The four fundamentals of M203 marksmanship are steady position, aiming, breathing, and trigger control. Only the first fundamental (steady position) varies. The other three remain the same regardless of the soldier's position.

a. **Steady Position.** This varies according to the position and the type of sight used (quadrant or leaf).

(1) ***Prone Position.*** When firing prone, a supported position is best.

(a) *Quadrant Sight* (Figure 5-1, page 5-2).

- Lie face down, grasp the M16 pistol magazine with your right hand, and place the butt of the rifle into the pocket of your right shoulder.
- Lower your right elbow to the ground so your shoulders are level. This places the weight of your body behind the weapon, which enables you to recover quickly each time you fire.

- Grasp the barrel grip with your left hand, supporting with sandbags. Straighten your upper body and spread your legs a comfortable distance apart. Try to point your toes outward and relax your ankles so your heels will rest on the ground. Relax the weight of your upper body forward onto your left arm.

Figure 5-1. Prone supported position, quadrant sight.

(a) *Leaf Sight* (Figure 5-2).
- While firing with the leaf sight at ranges greater than 150 meters, place the butt stock of the weapon under your armpit and grip firmly to prevent the weapon from moving.
- Lean your head 45 degrees to the right and place the M16 front sight post on the desired range. Raise the butt stock and lower the muzzle to obtain the proper sight alignment and sight picture.

WARNING
Ensure the sling is clear of the weapon muzzle before firing.

Figure 5-2. Prone supported position, leaf sight.

(2) ***Kneeling Position***.

(a) *Quadrant Sight* (Figure 5-3).

- Kneel on your right knee while facing the target with your right hand on the magazine and your left hand grasping the barrel grip.
- Place your left foot about .45 meter (18 inches) to your left front with your toes pointing in the general direction of the target.
- Keeping your right toe in place, sit on your right heel.
- Place your left elbow forward of your left knee, resting the flat portion of your upper arm on your knee.
- Move the rifle butt into the pocket of your right shoulder, pulling the rifle magazine with your right hand and grasping the barrel grip with your left hand.
- With your right hand on the rifle magazine, place your right forefinger in the trigger guard of the grenade launcher.
- Pull the rifle firmly into your shoulder.
- Pull your right elbow in close to your body to help you apply rearward pressure to the weapon. Ensure that your leg completes a solid, three-point base for your position.

Figure 5-3. Kneeling position, quadrant sight.

(b) *Leaf Sight* (Figure 5-4).

- For ranges greater than 150 meters, place the butt stock of the weapon under your armpit and grip firmly to prevent the weapon from moving.
- Lean your head 45 degrees to the right and place the front sight post of the M16 on the desired range. Raise the butt stock and lower the muzzle to obtain the proper sight alignment and sight picture.

Figure 5-4. Kneeling position, leaf sight.

(3) ***Sitting Position, Open-Legged.***

(a) *Quadrant Sight* (Figure 5-5).

- Sit down, breaking your fall with your right hand, and slide your buttocks well to the rear. Face the target half right, and spread your feet wide.
- Grasp the rifle magazine with your right hand and the barrel grip with your left hand.
- Bend forward from your hips.
- Move the butt of the rifle into the pocket of your right shoulder, still holding the rifle magazine with your right hand.

- Pull the weapon down slightly with your left hand and pull it to the rear firmly with your right hand.

Figure 5-5. Sitting position, open-legged, quadrant sight.

(b) *Leaf Sight* (Figure 5-6, page 5-6).
- For ranges greater than 150 meters, place the butt stock of the weapon under your armpit and grip firmly to prevent the weapon from moving.

- Lean your head 45 degrees to the right and place the M16 front sight post on the desired range. Raise the butt and lower the muzzle to obtain the proper sight alignment and sight picture.

Figure 5-6. Sitting position, open-legged, leaf sight.

(4) *Sitting Position, Cross-Ankle*.

(a) *Quadrant Sight* (Figure 5-7).

- Sit facing the target half right.
- Extend your legs from your body and cross your left ankle over your right ankle.
- Keep both ankles straight.
- Grasp the rifle magazine with your right hand and the barrel grip with your left.

- Place your left upper arm across your left knee.
- Move the butt of the rifle into the pocket of your right shoulder.

Figure 5-7. Sitting position, cross-ankled, quadrant sight.

(b) *Leaf Sight* (Figure 5-8).

- For ranges greater than 150 meters, place the butt stock of the weapon under your armpit and grip firmly to prevent the weapon from moving.
- Lean your head 45 degrees to the right and place the M16 front sight post on the desired range. Raise the butt and lower the muzzle to obtain the proper sight alignment and sight picture.

Figure 5-8. Sitting position, cross-ankled, leaf sight.

(5) *Sitting Position, Cross-Legged.*
(a) *Quadrant Sight* (Figure 5-9).

- Sit down facing the target half right.
- Cross your left leg over your right leg and draw both feet close to your body.
- Grasp the rifle magazine with your right hand.
- Move the butt of the rifle into the pocket of your right shoulder, and grasp the rifle barrel grip properly with your left hand.

Figure 5-9. Sitting position, cross-legged, quadrant sight.

(b) *Leaf Sight* (Figure 5-10).

- For ranges greater than 150 meters, place the butt stock of the weapon under your armpit and grip firmly to prevent the weapon from moving.
- Lean your head 45 degrees to the right and place the M16 front sight post on the desired range. Raise the butt and lower the muzzle to obtain the proper sight alignment and sight picture.

Figure 5-10. Sitting position, cross-legged, leaf sight.

(6) *Squatting Position.*

(a) *Quadrant Sight* (Figure 5-11).

- Turn half right to the target and, keeping both feet flat on the ground and a comfortable distance apart, squat as low as you can.
- Grasp the rifle magazine with your right hand.
- Place your left upper arm inside your left knee and the butt of the rifle into the pocket of your right shoulder. Grasp the rifle barrel grip properly.
- Lower your right elbow against the inside of your right knee.

Figure 5-11. Squatting position, quadrant sight.

(b) *Leaf Sight* (Figure 5-12).

- For ranges greater than 150 meters, place the butt stock of the weapon under your armpit and grip firmly to prevent the weapon from moving.
- Lean your head 45 degrees to the right and place the M16 front sight post on the desired range. Raise the butt and lower the muzzle to obtain proper sight alignment and sight picture.

Figure 5-12. Squatting position, leaf sight.

(7) *Fighting Position*.

(a) *Quadrant Sight*. If possible, use support when firing from a fighting position (Figure 5-13).

- Place your right foot against the rear of the fighting position and lean forward until your chest is against its forward edge.

- Grasp the magazine with your right hand.
- Place your left elbow on or against solid support.
- Use your right hand to position the butt of the rifle in the pocket of your right shoulder. Grasp the rifle barrel grip properly.
- Place your right elbow on or against a solid support and relax into a comfortable firing position.

NOTE: The weapon must not touch the support.

Figure 5-13. Fighting position, quadrant sight.

(b) *Leaf Sight* (Figure 5-14).
- For ranges greater than 150 meters, place the butt stock of the weapon under your armpit and grip firmly to prevent the weapon from moving.
- Lean your head 45 degrees to the right and place the M16 front sight post on the desired range. Raise the butt and lower the muzzle to obtain proper sight alignment and sight picture.

Figure 5-14. Fighting position, leaf sight.

(8) *Standing Position.*
(a) *Quadrant Sight* (Figure 5-15).
- Face the target while standing with your feet spread a comfortable distance apart.
- Grasp the rifle barrel grip with your left hand and the rifle magazine with your right hand.
- Place the butt of the stock into your right shoulder so that the sight is level with your eyes.
- Hold your right elbow high to form a good pocket for the butt of the stock and to permit a strong rearward pressure with your right hand.
- Hold most of the weight of the weapon with your left hand.

- Shift your feet until you achieve a natural aiming stance.

Figure 5-15. Standing position, quadrant sight.

(a) *Leaf Sight* (Figure 5-16).
- For ranges greater than 150 meters, place the butt stock of the weapon under your armpit and grip firmly to prevent the weapon from moving.
- Lean your head 45 degrees to the right and place the M16 front sight post on the desired range. Raise the butt and lower the muzzle to obtain the proper sight alignment and sight picture.

Figure 5-16. Standing position, leaf sight.

b. **Aiming**. Aiming procedures for every position are as follows:

(1) *Aligning Sight*. When using the leaf sight, align it with the front sight post of the M16. When using the quadrant sight, align its rear sight aperture with its front sight post. Picture a horizontal line through the center of the leaf sight or rear sight aperture: the top of the M16's front sight post should touch this line. Picture a vertical line through the center of the leaf sight or rear sight aperture: this line should vertically bisect the front sight post (Figure 5-17).

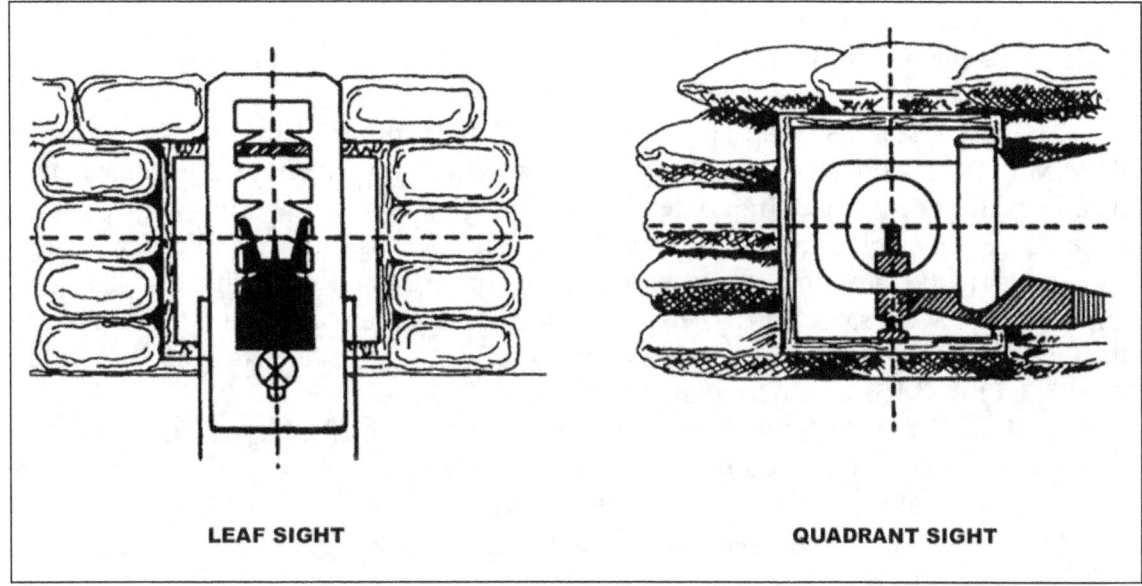

LEAF SIGHT   **QUADRANT SIGHT**

Figure 5-17. Sight pictures for leaf and quadrant sights.

(2) *Focusing*. For either sight, focus on the front sight post. A good firing position places your eye directly on line with the center of the leaf sight or rear sight aperture. Your eye's natural ability to center objects in a circle and seek the point of greatest light will help you align the sight correctly.

(3) *Obtaining Sight Picture*. To achieve a correct sight picture, align the front sight post and the leaf sight or rear sight aperture with the target. For area targets, aim where the round's bursting radius will make the round most effective. For point targets, aim at the target's center of mass.

c. **Breathing**. The technique for breathing is the same for every position: Breathe naturally, exhale most of your air, hold your breath, and fire before you become uncomfortable. In combat, just choke off your breath before firing.

d. **Trigger Control**. The technique for trigger control is the same for every position. Place your trigger finger (the index finger of your right hand) so that the trigger is between the first joint and the tip of your finger (not at the extreme end of your finger). Adjust for your hand size and grip. Then, squeeze your trigger finger to the rear without disturbing the lay of the weapon.

5-2. LIMITED VISIBILITY

The fundamentals of marksmanship are almost the same in limited visibility as in normal visibility.

a. **Steady Position**. An M203 with an AN/PVS-4 mounted on it leans to the left. When assuming a steady position, the grenadier must apply more rearward pressure to compensate for the lean and then steady the weapon.

b. **Aiming**. The grenadier sights with the reticle of the AN/PVS-4 rather than with the M203's iron sights. Sighting this way requires him to change position, which breaks his stock weld and makes the weapon seem heavier.

c. **Breathing**. Though breathing itself is affected little by limited visibility, using night vision devices that magnify the field of view increases the effect of weapon movement caused by breathing.

d. **Trigger Control**. This is the same regardless of visibility conditions. The objective is to keep the weapon aligned with the target.

e. **Night Vision Devices**. The AN/PVS-7 is issued for use with the M203, whereas the AN/PVS-4 is normally issued for use with crew-served weapons. M203 gunners may qualify with either device. In a defensive position, the gunner identifies targets during daylight and constructs aiming or elevation stakes. Because the AN/PVS-7 rear sight must be set to the far setting to sense rounds, the gunner cannot see both the M203 sights and the target at the same time. Therefore, stakes are more important with the AN/PVS-7 than with the AN/PVS-4. (On the rear sight of the M16A1, the far setting is "L." On the rear sight of the M16A2, the far setting is "02.")

f. **Marked-Sling Method**. The best field-expedient method for firing the M203 grenade launcher in limited visibility is the marked-sling method using only the M16 rifle series (Figure 5-18). To use this method, the grenadier must--

(1) Face the target and kneel on the right knee (if firing right-handed), keeping the left foot pointed toward the target.

(2) Loosen the sling and place the forward foot in the sling.

(3) Place the butt of the stock firmly on the ground.

(4) Using the left hand, grasp firmly the upper barrel grip just below the barrel.

(5) Grasp the receiver group with the right hand.

Figure 5-18. Marked-sling method.

WARNING
Placing the knee against the buttstock can cause injury.

---

(6) Ensure the sling is taut and vertical between the front sling swivel and the boot (Figure 5-19). If not, the rounds will impact at a greater range than desired.

Figure 5-19. Front-sling swivel and front of boot.

(7) Fire several rounds to determine the desired range.

(8) Mark the sling (where it is held to the ground by the foot) with colored tape, paint, ink, or whatever is available. Mark the position of the buckles (Figure 5-20) so that, if either is moved, the grenadier can return them to their original positions and be assured of constant range accuracy.

Figure 5-20. Marked sling and buckle highlighted.

(9) If the sling gets wet, it may stretch or shrink, indirectly causing the rounds to impact closer or farther than desired.

5-3. NBC ENVIRONMENT

The fundamentals of marksmanship remain valid in the NBC environment, but some modifications may be needed to accommodate the equipment.

a. **Steady Position**. Bulky NBC wear requires the grenadier to press the stock of the weapon more firmly into his shoulder pocket.

b. **Aiming**. Aiming is affected little by NBC.

c. **Breathing**. Wearing the protective mask makes breathing more difficult. Grenadiers must try to breathe normally to avoid hyperventilating while firing.

d. **Trigger Control**. All soldiers must wear rubber gloves.

5-4. FIRE COMMANDS

Standard fire commands are explained to grenadiers and are used during all subsequent gunnery training. Trainers give the appropriate elements before each dry-fire or live-fire exercise. The grenadier performs as directed and repeats each element as it is announced. (Chapter 6 provides a detailed explanation of fire commands.)

a. **Alert**. The trainer gives the alert as a fire mission. On hearing this, the grenadier loads the weapon and moves the safety lever to FIRE.

b. **Direction**. The trainer gives the direction to target.

c. **Description**. The trainer describes the target, for example, BUNKER or MACHINE GUN POSITION, and the grenadier lays on the target.

d. **Range**. The trainer gives the (estimated) range to the target, for example, "150."

e. **Method of Fire**. The method of fire for either target is three rounds. On the basic range, grenadiers fire at both point and area targets.

f. **Command to Open Fire**. To open fire, the trainer commands COMMENCE FIRING or AT MY COMMAND. When ready, the grenadier announces UP and fires or waits for the command to fire. When all grenadiers are ready, the trainer gives the actual command to fire.

5-5. DRY-FIRE EXERCISES

Dry-fire exercises train grenadiers in the techniques of loading, unloading, immediate action, fundamentals of marksmanship, and sight manipulation. These exercises are conducted with TP or dummy rounds. The trainer gives fire commands as appropriate.

a. **Loading and Unloading Exercise**. This trains the grenadier to operate and clear the weapon proficiently. Loading and unloading procedures (Chapter 2) should be practiced with dummy ammunition.

b. **Immediate Action Exercise**. This exercise is conducted with a dummy round and the basic grenade launcher target.

(1) Load the weapon with a dummy round and aim it at one of the targets on the basic grenade launcher range.

(2) Maintain the sight picture while you pull the trigger to simulate firing.

(3) When you are informed that you have a misfire, apply misfire procedures; then continue to fire (Chapter 4).

c. **Aiming Exercise**. This exercise requires the grenadier to simulate firing a dummy round at a target on the basic grenade launcher range.

(1) Maintain your sight picture throughout the firing cycle.

(2) If, after firing, you note that the sight picture has moved, then you were unsteady when you fired.

(3) After each shot, apply immediate action procedures to extract and eject the dummy cartridges. Then recock the barrel assembly.

d. **Sight Setting and Sight Changing Exercises**. These exercises train the grenadier to operate and adjust both quadrant and leaf sights.

(1) *Range*. Manipulate the sights to different range settings (quadrant sight, 50 to 400 meters; leaf sight, 50 to 250 meters). To learn to make fine adjustments for elevation, manipulate the sights from the minimum to the maximum setting. When you do not have time to adjust the sights, you may adjust the aiming point instead.

(2) *Windage*. Depress the rear sight aperture left and right and traverse the windage screw across the entire scale.

e. **Dry-Fire Proficiency (Performance) Exam**. Grenadiers practice the dry-fire tasks until they become proficient in operating the weapon; then they take the dry-fire proficiency exam (Appendix C). This exam emphasizes learning by doing. Before he can progress to live firing, each grenadier must demonstrate skill in every task in the exam.

f. **Remedial Training**. Soldiers who do not pass the performance exam must attend remedial training, after which they are retested. The soldiers who pass may help train those having difficulty.

5-6. SENSING AND ADJUSTMENT OF FIRE

The grenadier determines (senses) where the grenade landed relative to the target and then adjusts elevation and deflection.

a. **Sensing**. As soon as the grenade explodes, determine where it exploded with respect to the target. This is called "sensing" (the impact) and has two aspects: range and deviation. Because the casualty radius of the HE round is 5 meters (5 1/2 yards), determine both range and deviation to the nearest 5 meters.

(1) *Range*. Sense the range as one of the following:

(a) *Short*. The grenade bursts between you and the target.

(b) *Over*. The grenade bursts beyond the target.

(c) *Target*. The grenade hits any part of the target.

(d) *Range Correct*. The grenade bursts slightly left or right of the target, but at the correct range.

(e) *Doubtful*. The grenade burst left or right of the grenadier, but you cannot sense the range.

(2) *Deviation*. Announce a deviation sensing as either--

- Right or left of the target, or
- On line with the target.

b. **Adjustment of Fire**. To ensure a second-round hit, adjust your fire by sensing the impact of the round and manipulating the sight.

(1) If time allows, whether using the AN/PVS-4 or AN/PVS-7, adjust the sights; if time is critical, adjust the point of aim instead.

(2) If the grenade lands more than 25 meters over or short of the target, adjust the range quadrant to bring the next grenade on target.

(3) If the grenade explodes less than 25 meters from the target, adjust the point of aim to bring the next grenade on target.

(4) If the launcher is properly zeroed, deviation errors are normally small and easily corrected by adjusting the aiming point. A wind strong enough to move the grenade out of its normal trajectory, however, increases the size of the deviation errors. After observing the effect of the wind on the strike of the grenade, compensate for the effect of the wind by aiming into it. This should help bring the next grenade on target. For example, if the grenade bursts to the left and short of the target, sense the strike of the round relative to the target and then adjust an equivalent distance to the right and over the target to achieve a target hit. Watch the flight of the grenade to the target. This helps determine the effect of the wind on the grenade as it moves toward the target. Evaluating and compensating for the wind before firing increases your chances of achieving a first-round hit.

5-7. GRENADE LAUNCHER RANGE LAYOUT

The grenade launcher range is designed for all grenade launchers. Because soldiers can qualify on this range in all conditions, it prepares grenadiers for combat situations. The range has four stations (Figure 5-21). Minimum range personnel and their duties are the same for M203 qualification firing as they are for other grenadier firing. These personnel include an OIC, NCOIC, safety officer, ammunition NCO, tower operator, station NCOs, primary trainer, and concurrent training trainers. However, local policy may require more personnel. (Appendix D discusses range safety; TC 25-8 provides a detailed setup and target configuration for this range.)

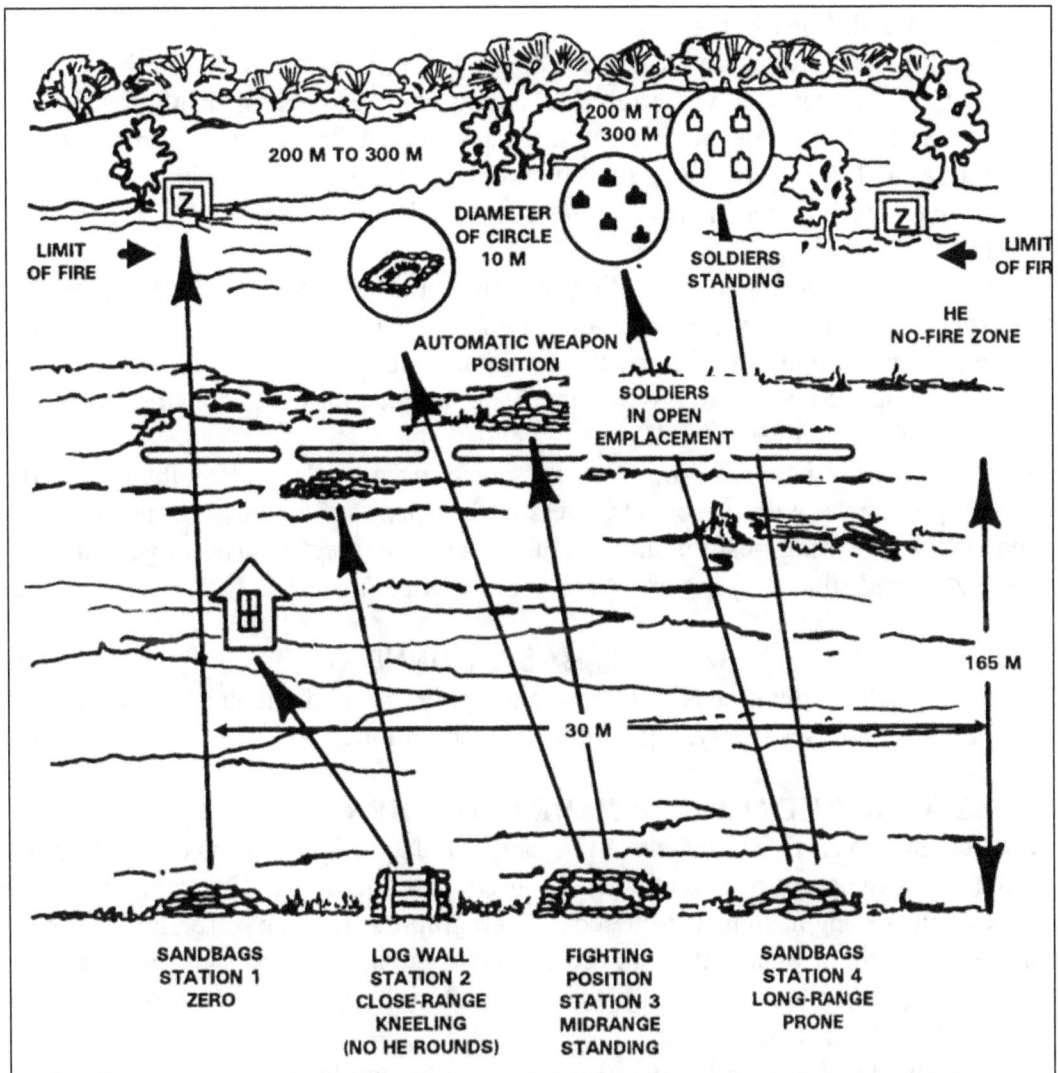

Figure 5-21. Grenade launcher range.

5-8. DESCRIPTION OF RANGE AND TARGETS

The range has four self-contained stations. It is 30 meters wide by 500 meters deep and has a no-HE fire zone out to 130 meters. (Grenadiers can fire HE only on Stations 1, 3, and 4.) Targets should be built from durable materials to reduce downrange target maintenance. Those within each station must be grouped and spaced so that the grenadier may fire on close-range, mid-range, and long-range targets, in that order. The following description of the stations and targets is included to help trainers maintain control during zeroing, practice, and record fire.

NOTE: To simplify the task of finding and destroying duds, trainers must ensure the impact area is free of any vegetation other than short grass.

a. Station 1 consists of a prone fighting position with a log or sandbag support and a zeroing target at 200 meters. The target should be constructed of logs or other suitable material. It must have a surface at least 2 meters high by 2 meters wide (6 feet by 6 feet). The target should be clearly marked with a large "Z" painted in a color that contrasts with the surrounding background and that is visible in different sun or glare conditions.

b. Station 2 consists of an upright log or log wall, a kneeling firing position about 4 feet high, and 2 point-type targets. The targets include a simulated window or door of a building at 90 to 100 meters and a small bunker or fighting position with overhead cover at 125 meters. The targets may be constructed of logs, sandbags, or other suitable material.

c. Station 3 consists of a fighting position and two targets. The targets are a two-person bunker at 150 meters and an automatic weapon position at 175 meters. The bunker represents a point target, and the automatic weapon position represents a target that can be engaged with area-type fire. The targets may be constructed of logs, sandbags, or other suitable material.

d. Station 4 consists of a prone fighting position with a log or sandbag support and two area-type targets (with personnel targets in the open) at 250 and 350 meters. The log or sandbags at the firing position are used for support and cover. The targets are E-type and F-type shaped silhouette and are made out of durable materials.

Section II. BASIC GUNNERY

Basic gunnery allows the grenadier to zero and apply the fundamentals of marksmanship during live-fire exercises in day, night, and NBC conditions.

5-9. ZEROING THE M203 GRENADE LAUNCHER

A correct zero consists of the elevation and windage sight settings that enable the grenadier to hit the point of aim at a given range with one of the three sighting systems: leaf, quadrant, or night sight (discussed in paragraph 5-13). To zero the M203 using either the leaf sight or quadrant sight, the grenadier engages a target at 200 meters. (The M203 is normally zeroed using only the quadrant sight, but may be zeroed with both sights or with only the leaf sight.)

a. **Zeroing the Leaf Sight**. A red mark at 50 meters on the leaf sight reminds the grenadier not to zero at this range.

(1) Select a target at 200 meters.

(2) Place the sight in the upright position.

(3) Place the center mark of the windage scale on the index line on the rear of the sight base.

(4) Loosen the elevation adjustment screw on the leaf sight.

(5) Place the leaf sight's index line on the sight mount's center elevation mark.

(6) Tighten the elevation adjustment screw.

(7) Assume a prone supported firing position.

(8) Load one round of 40-mm HE or TP ammunition.

(9) Use correct sighting and aiming procedures to align the target with the front leaf sight.

(10) Fire a round, sense the impact, and adjust the sight.

(a) *Windage*. Turn the sight windage screw clockwise to move the leaf sight to the left and vice versa. One increment moves round impact 1 1/2 meters at a range of 200 meters.

(b) *Range*. Use a 40-mm cartridge case and turn the elevation adjustment screw to raise the leaf sight (this increases range) or to lower the leaf sight (this decreases range). Turning the screw one increment moves round impact 10 meters at a range of 200 meters.

(11) Fire two more cartridges, readjusting the sight after each. Once a round impacts within 5 meters of the target, the weapon is zeroed.

(12) After you have zeroed the weapon, record the zero data on your scorecard. As soon as you can, transfer the information to a small piece of paper and tape this inside the M16 pistol grip.

b. **Zeroing the Quadrant Sight**.

(1) Select a target at 200 meters.

(2) Ensure that the quadrant sight is correctly mounted on the rifle's carrying handle.

(3) Open the front sight post and rear sight aperture.

(a) Move the front sight post to its highest position and then back 2 1/2 turns.

(b) Depress the rear sight retainer. Slide the rear sight aperture to the left until its white index line aligns with the edge of the sight aperture arm.

(4) Move the sight latch rearward and reposition the quadrant sight arm to zeroing range (200 meters).

(5) Assume a prone supported firing position.

(6) Use correct sighting and aiming procedures to align the target with the front sight post and rear sight aperture.

(7) Load one round of 40-mm HE or TP ammunition.

(8) Fire a round, sense the impact, and adjust the sight.

(a) *Elevation*. Turn the front sight post right (to decrease elevation) or left (to increase elevation). At a range of 200 meters, one full turn equals 5 meters.

(b) *Windage*. Press the sight aperture retainer. Move the rear sight aperture away from the barrel to move the trajectory to the left or vice versa. At a range of 200 meters, one notch on the rear sight aperture equals 1 1/2 meters.

(9) Fire two more cartridges, readjusting the sights after each. If the round lands within 5 meters of the target, the weapon is zeroed.

(10) After you have zeroed the weapon, record the zero data on your scorecard. As soon as you can, transfer this information to a small piece of paper and tape this inside the M16 pistol grip.

5-10. OVERALL QUALIFICATION STANDARDS

DA Form 2946-R (40-mm Grenade Launcher Scorecard) is used for qualification firing. To qualify with an M203, a grenadier must perform to prescribed standards and must score at least 60 of 90 possible points. Each target hit is worth 10 points. Zeroing is not included on the scorecard because the weapon must be zeroed before qualification firing. However, the zero data should already have been entered on the scorecard when the weapon was zeroed. HE familiarization may be included in qualification firing but is not scored. Ratings are awarded based on the point chart shown on the scorecard. A blank scorecard is provided in back of this field manual and must be locally reproduced on 8 1/2- by 11-inch paper. Figure 5-22 shows an example of a completed scorecard.

40-MM GRENADE LAUNCHER SCORECARD

For use of this form see FM 3-22.31, Chapter 5; the proponent agency is TRADOC.

DATA REQUIRED BY THE PRIVACY ACT OF 1974

AUTHORITY: 10 USC 3012(g)/Executive Order 9397.

PRINCIPAL PURPOSE(S): Record individual performance.

ROUTINE USES: Evaluate individual proficiency and determine proficiency level. SSN is used for positive identification purposes only.

DISCLOSURE: Voluntary. Individuals not providing information cannot be rated or scored on a mass basis.

NAME: _Rager, Ronald_   QUALIFICATION RATING: _Expert_

SSN: _XXX-XX-XXX_   DATE: _12 Apr 2000_   GRADE: _E-5_

ORGANIZATION: _CSC 2/2 INF_   ZERO LEAF SIGHT: DEFILADE _____ ELEVATION _____   ZERO QUADRANT SIGHT: DEFILADE _L4_ ELEVATION _R1_

TASK NUMBER	DAY AND NBC RECORD FIRE	TIME
1	TGT 1 HIT _X_ MISS _____ POINTS _10_ TGT 2 HIT _X_ MISS _____ POINTS _10_	2 MIN
2	TGT 1 HIT _____ MISS _X_ POINTS _0_ TGT 2 HIT _X_ MISS _____ POINTS _10_	2 MIN
3	TGT 1 HIT _X_ MISS _____ POINTS _10_ TGT 2 HIT _X_ MISS _____ POINTS _10_	2 MIN
4	HIT _X_ MISS _____ POINTS _10_	2 MIN

TASK NUMBER	DAY AND NBC RECORD FIRE (CONT'D)	TIME
5	HIT _X_ MISS _____ POINTS _10_	2 MIN

TASK NUMBER	NIGHT RECORD FIRE	TIME
6	HIT _X_ MISS _____ POINTS _10_	2 MIN

TOTAL POINTS _80_

EXPERT	80 – 90
GRENADIER, FIRST CLASS	70 – 75
GRENADIER, SECOND CLASS	60 – 65
UNQUALIFIED	0 – 55

GRADER'S SIGNATURE _Daniel Sellers_

OIC'S SIGNATURE _Billy Greer_

DA FORM 2946-R, NOV 2002   EDITION OF AUG 94 IS OBSOLETE   USAPA V1.00ES

Figure 5-22. Example completed DA Form 2946-R, 40-mm Grenade Launcher Scorecard.

5-11. DAY RECORD FIRE

Day record fire gives the grenadier the confidence and experience he needs to progress from dry-fire exercises to record fire. All soldiers must be prepared to accomplish their missions, even in protective clothing; thus, day record fire includes two NBC tasks (Tasks 4 and 5). This exercise is conducted on a grenade launcher range IAW Firing Table I (Table 5-1). Before they fire for qualification, grenadiers must first zero their weapons and receive instruction on the objectives, range, targets, and qualification standards. The unit is organized in firing orders based on range constraints. Each firing order consists of two grenadiers, one of whom assists. Grenadiers fire this exercise from the following fighting positions: kneeling supported, mid-range supported, long-range supported, NBC mid-range point target, and NBC mid-range area target. For each of these tasks, the grenadier can designate which target he will engage first.

WARNING

Before allowing anyone to move between stations, ensure that all rifles and grenade launchers have been cleared, bolts are to the rear, and barrel assemblies are in the open position. Anyone observing an unsafe act should call CEASE FIRE and notify range personnel immediately.

---

a. **Station 1, Zeroing.** The grenadier zeroes with both quadrant and leaf sights at Station 1.

(1) *Leaf Sight.* From a prone supported firing position, fire to zero the weapon. This reinforces the experience gained during dry firing and allows practice in loading and firing with the most accurate sensing and adjustments obtainable. If you zero in three rounds, use the other two rounds to confirm the zero. If you cannot zero with five rounds, the trainer must remove you from the firing line for remedial training.

(a) Prepare the sight for zeroing.

(b) Assume a good prone supported firing position.

(c) When you receive the following fire command, repeat each element as it is given:

GRENADIER
FRONT
200 (ZERO PANEL)
ONE ROUND
COMMENCE FIRING

(d) Load one round, obtain the proper sight picture, and announce UP to your assistant.

(e) When the tower operator gives the command to commence firing, fire one round at the panel marked "Z."

(f) Sense the impact of the round. If the round did not land within 5 meters of the zero panel, adjust the sights for windage and elevation.

(g) Repeat until a round lands within 5 meters of the zero panel.

(h) Once you have zeroed the weapon, record the zero data on your scorecard. As soon as you can, transfer the information to a small piece of paper and tape this inside the M16 pistol grip.

(2) *Quadrant Sight*. From a prone supported firing position, fire to zero the weapon. This reinforces the experience gained during dry firing and gives you practice in loading and firing with the most accurate sensing and adjustments you can obtain. The steps for zeroing with the quadrant sight are the same as those for zeroing with the leaf sight.

b. **Station 2, Task 1, Kneeling Position**. (Only TP rounds may be used at this station.)

(1) When you receive the command DESIGNATE THE TARGET, identify the target you intend to engage by announcing WINDOW or BUNKER.

(2) When you receive the command DETERMINE THE RANGE, announce the range to the target.

(3) Load one of the three rounds allotted. Because HE must not be fired at ranges of less than 165 meters on the basic grenade launcher range, use only TP rounds.

(4) When you receive the following fire command, repeat each element as it is given:

> GRENADIER
> FRONT
> 3 ROUNDS
> 100 (window) or 115 (bunker)
> COMMENCE FIRING

(5) Acquire the proper sight picture and announce UP to the grader.

(6) Engage the target given in the fire command until you hit it. Fire any remaining rounds at the second target. You need no other fire command. For each round you fire, your assistant announces HIT or MISS.

Task	Time	Rounds	Type	Target and Range
1	2 minutes	3	TP	Window at 90 to 100 meters; bunker at 105 to 115 meters.
2	2 minutes	3	TP	Bunker at 135 to 150 meters; automatic weapon at 200 to 250 meters.
3	2 minutes	3	TP	Troops in open emplacement at 275 to 300 meters; troops in open at 325 to 350 meters.
4	2 minutes	3	TP	Bunker at 135 to 150 meters.
5	2 minutes	3	TP	Automatic weapon at 200 to 250 meters.

Table 5-1. Firing Table I, day record fire qualification.

c. **Station 3, Task 2, Mid-Range Position**.

(1) When you receive the command DESIGNATE THE TARGET, identify the target you intend to engage by announcing BUNKER or AUTOMATIC WEAPON.

(2) When you receive the command DETERMINE THE RANGE, announce the range to the target.

(3) Load one of the three rounds allotted.

(4) When you receive the following fire command, repeat each element as it is given:

> GRENADIER
> FRONT
> 3 ROUNDS
> 150 (bunker) or 250 (automatic weapon)
> COMMENCE FIRING

(5) Acquire the proper sight picture and announce UP to the grader.

(6) Engage the target given in the fire command until you hit it. Fire any remaining rounds at the second target. You need no other fire command. For each round you fire, your assistant announces HIT or MISS.

d. **Station 4, Task 3, Long-Range Supported Position**.

(1) When you receive the command DESIGNATE THE TARGET, identify the target you intend to engage by announcing TROOPS IN THE OPEN EMPLACEMENT or TROOPS IN THE OPEN.

(2) When you receive the command DETERMINE THE RANGE, announce the range to the target.

(3) Load one of the three rounds allotted.

(4) When you receive the following fire command, repeat each element as it is given:

> GRENADIER
> FRONT
> 3 ROUNDS
> 300 (troops in the open)
> COMMENCE FIRING

(5) Acquire the proper sight picture, and announce UP to the grader.

(6) When the tower operator gives the command to FIRE, engage the target given in the fire command until you hit it. Fire any remaining rounds at the second target. You need no other fire command. Before firing, you must know the procedure to follow in the event of a stoppage. For each round you fire, your assistant announces HIT or MISS.

e. **Station 3, Task 4, Mid-Range Position, Point Target, NBC**.

(1) Put on, clear, and check your mask within 9 seconds. Within the next 6 seconds, pull the hood over your head and zip the front of it closed.

(2) Load one of the three rounds allotted.

(3) When you receive the following fire command, repeat each element as it is given:

> FIRE MISSION
> FRONT

3 ROUNDS
150 (bunker)
AT MY COMMAND

(4) Acquire the proper sight picture and announce UP to your assistant.

(5) Have your assistant signal the tower operator that you are ready.

(6) When the tower operator gives the command to commence firing, engage the target given in the fire command until you hit it. For each round you fire, your assistant announces HIT or MISS.

   f. **Station 3, Task 5, Mid-Range Position, Area Target, NBC**.

(1) Load one of the three rounds allotted.

(2) When you receive the following fire command, repeat each element as it is given:

FIRE MISSION
FRONT
3 ROUNDS
200 (automatic weapon position)
AT MY COMMAND

(3) Acquire the proper sight picture and announce UP to your assistant.

(4) Have your assistant signal the tower operator that you are ready.

(5) When the tower operator gives the command to FIRE, engage the target given in the fire command until you hit it. For each round you fire, your assistant announces HIT or MISS.

5-12. DAY RECORD FIRE QUALIFICATION STANDARDS

Before qualification firing, each grenadier must know the tasks, the time and ammunition required, the procedures to follow if a stoppage occurs, the penalties for failure to stop firing when commanded or signaled to do so, and the method used for scoring targets.

   a. **Time and Ammunition**. Each grenadier determines the target and its distance before loading any rounds. When the grenadier receives the command to FIRE, the time allotted for that task in Firing Table I begins.

   b. **Stoppages**. The grenadier must apply immediate action procedures if a stoppage occurs. If he can reduce the stoppage, he can continue to fire the course. The trainers allow the grenadier an extra 15 seconds for each application of immediate action.

(1) If a stoppage occurs that you cannot reduce by immediate action, raise your hand and announce TIME.

(2) When you say TIME, the assistant trainer notes the time, ensures that a real stoppage exists, and tries to clear the stoppage. If he clears it, you can complete firing. If he is unable to clear it, the grader will clear it, and you will be allowed 15 seconds for each round remaining to complete firing.

(3) If you made an error that caused the stoppage, you do not receive extra time, and your score consists only of whatever you had earned when the stoppage occurred.

(4) If the grenade launcher must be replaced, you are allotted 10 rounds to zero a new one; then you may repeat the exercise.

(5) If malfunctions prevent you from finishing the exercise in the time allowed, you can finish it in an "alibi run" after all other grenadiers complete firing.

c. **Penalties**. Five points are deducted from the score of any grenadier who fails to stop firing when the trainer commands or signals to do so. If a grenadier fires at the wrong target, he loses the rounds allotted for the other target, which leaves him only the remainder of his rounds to expend on both targets.

d. **Target Scoring**. The trainer or assistant trainer records scores on DA Form 2946-R. They determine whether each grenade fired is a hit or miss and assign 0 points for a miss or 10 points for a hit. Tasks 1 through 3 each consist of two targets, so the total available for each of these tasks is 20 points. The grenadier may select which of the two targets to engage first. If he scores a hit on the first, the trainer permits him to engage the second. Once he hits both targets, he returns any unexpended rounds to the assistant trainer. Tasks 4 and 5 each consist of firing one target for a total of 10 points each.

(1) *Window or Door*. To score a hit on a window or door, the grenade must either strike the target or go through the opening in the center of the target.

(2) *Bunker*. To score a hit on a bunker, the grenade must strike anywhere on the face of the bunker.

(3) *Automatic Weapon*. To score a hit on an automatic weapon, the grenade must strike within 5 meters of the target.

(4) *Troops*. To score a hit on troops, the grenade must strike within 5 meters of the target.

5-13. MOUNTING THE AN/PVS-4 (WITHOUT THE RAIL SYSTEM)

The grenadier must mount the AN/PVS-4 to the weapon before he zeroes it, and he must do both before he can qualify with the M203 grenade launcher. To mount the scope, the grenadier must--

a. Remove the quadrant sight.

b. Position the mounting bracket assembly on the left side of the rifle so that the two clamps project through the opening under the handle. Loosen the wing nuts completely (Figure 5-23).

c. Turn the clamp plates so that the pointed ends are in the UP position and are seated against the handle.

d. Tighten the wing nuts clockwise until the mounting bracket is secure against the weapon.

e. Position the sight in the groove on top of the bracket and align the threaded hole in the base of the sight mounting adapter with the lever screw assembly. Tighten the screw clockwise firmly to secure the sight to the bracket.

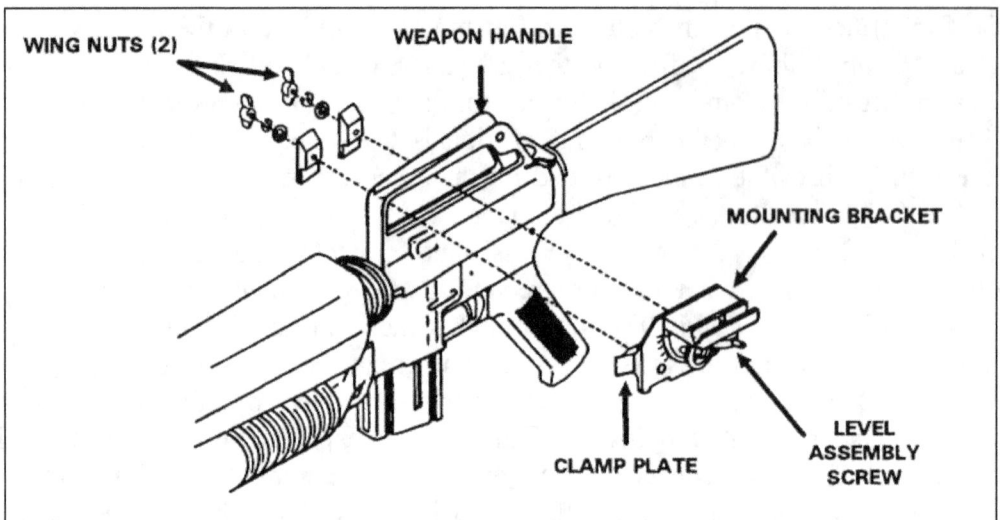

Figure 5-23. Installing the mounting bracket.

5-14. ZEROING THE AN/PVS-4 TO THE M203

After being mounted on the M203, the nightsight must be zeroed to the M16 before it can be zeroed to the M203. FM 23-9 provides instructions for doing this. The M16 is then used to zero the nightsight to the M203. The grenade launcher rounds are fired only to confirm the zero. To zero the nightsight to the M203--

a. **Center the Reticle Pattern**. Use the aiming points on the nightsight reticle (Figure 5-24, page 5-34) and the range settings on the mounting bracket. Center the nightsight's reticle pattern within the field of view (FOV). Note that it may not be centered even if it appears to be. To ensure it is, rotate the azimuth control knob either way until it stops. Then, rotate it back the opposite way, counting the number of clicks until it stops again (this may be any number of clicks between 200 and 600). Divide the number of clicks in half and rotate the knob in the original direction by that number of clicks. For example, if the total number of clicks is 500, rotate the knob back 250 clicks in the original direction. Center the elevation using the same procedure with the elevation control knob. The total amount of elevation clicks also varies between 200 and 600.

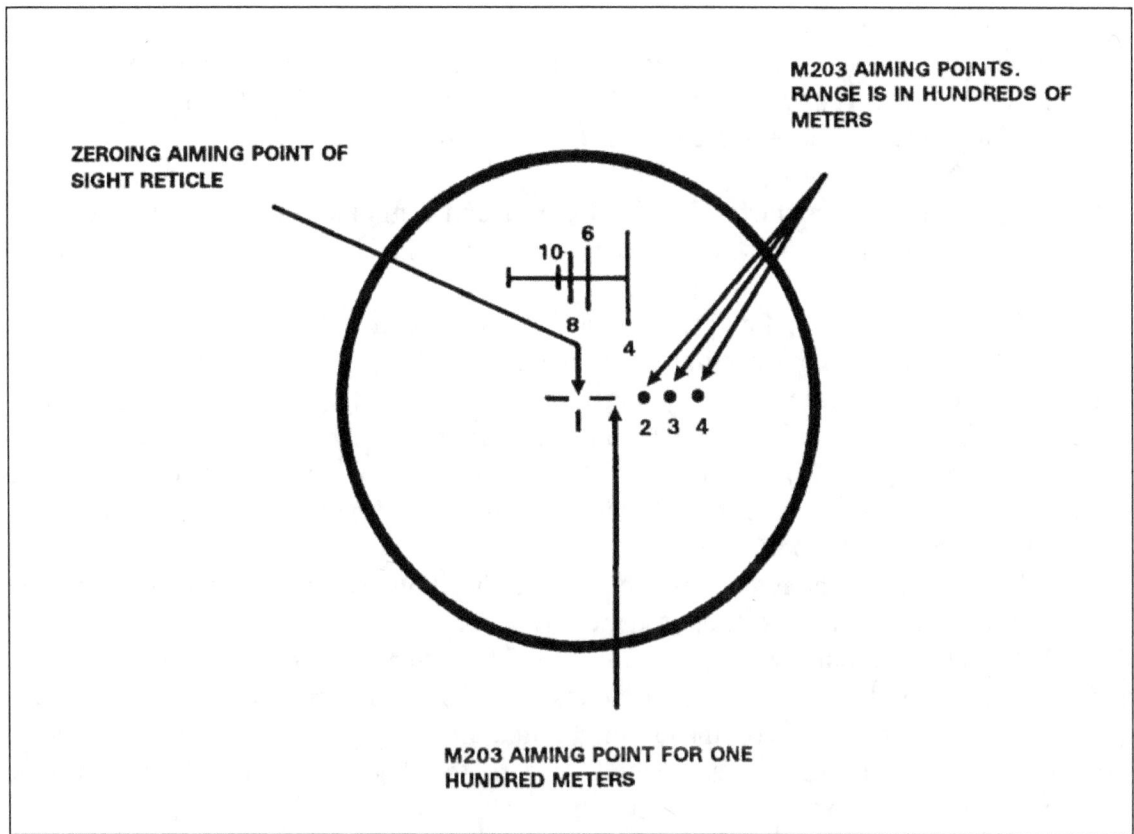

Figure 5-24. Aiming points.

b. **Adjust the Reticle Pattern**. Before adjusting the reticle pattern, the grenadier should fire three 5.56-mm rounds and then retighten the mount wing nuts to securely seat the sight. Once this is done, the grenadier fires at a 10-meter target because hitting and spotting this target is easier than hitting a 25-meter target. This procedure may be performed in daylight using the daylight cover:

(1) Turn the sight on and adjust the reticle intensity to the desired level of illumination.

(2) Place an M16 25-meter target at 10 meters and stabilize the weapon.

(3) Fire a 5.56-mm round at the center of the target and mark the hole the round makes.

(a) If the round misses the entire target, reseat the sight exactly as previously described.

(b) If the round hits the target but not within 20 centimeters (8 inches) of the center, adjust the azimuth and elevation controls to bring the impact point toward the center of the target. Then fire a second round. Continue to fire single rounds and adjust the controls until the rounds strike within the desired distance from the center.

(4) Once the reticle is adjusted, move the 25-meter target out to 25 meters and zero the grenade launcher. Do *not* remove the nightsight from the weapon until you have obtained a zero.

c. **Zero at 25 Meters**. This zero is not recorded. To obtain a 25-meter zero, the grenadier must—

(1) Stabilize the weapon.

(2) Center the reticle's zeroing range aiming point on the target aiming point, which is in the center of the target (Figure 5-21). Fire until you obtain a good three-round shot group. Triangulate and locate the center of the shot group.

NOTE: Even if the nightsight is dismounted and remounted on the same weapon, some changes in its zeroing will occur, so it must be zeroed again.

(3) Turn the azimuth and elevation control knobs to adjust the sight reticle. Move the center of the shot group 9.8 centimeters (3 7/8 inches) below and 4.2 centimeters (1 5/8 inches) to the right of the target aiming point (Figure 5-22). For example, if the shot group is high and to the left of the desired impact point, adjust the elevation down (DN) and the azimuth right (RT). One click of the azimuth or elevation adjustment moves the strike of the round .63 centimeter (1/4 inch) at a range of 25 meters. Two clicks move the reticle about one square on the target.

(4) After adjusting the reticle, assume a stable position. Place the reticle aiming point on the target aiming point and fire three more rounds.

(5) Repeat steps 3 and 4 until the rounds strike within a 3.2 centimeter (1 1/4 inch) circle in the desired location 9.8 centimeters (3 7/8 inches) below and 4.2 centimeters (1 5/8 inches) to the right of the aiming point, or until you have fired 12 rounds, whichever occurs first. If you are unable to zero the AN/PVS-4 after 12 rounds, the trainer must send you to remedial training.

(6) Confirm the zero on the grenade launcher range using a 200-meter target. Place the nightsight into operation and use its reticle, which has two parts. Use the vertical line in the upper part of the reticle to estimate range and the lower part to aim the weapon.

(a) Set the range as estimated on the range indicator of the mounting bracket (Figure 5-21).

(b) Engage the target, placing the aiming point of the sight reticle on the target's center of mass (Figure 5-25, page 5-36). Fire the weapon using all your marksmanship skills. You have confirmed the zero if two of three rounds strike within 5 meters of the target.

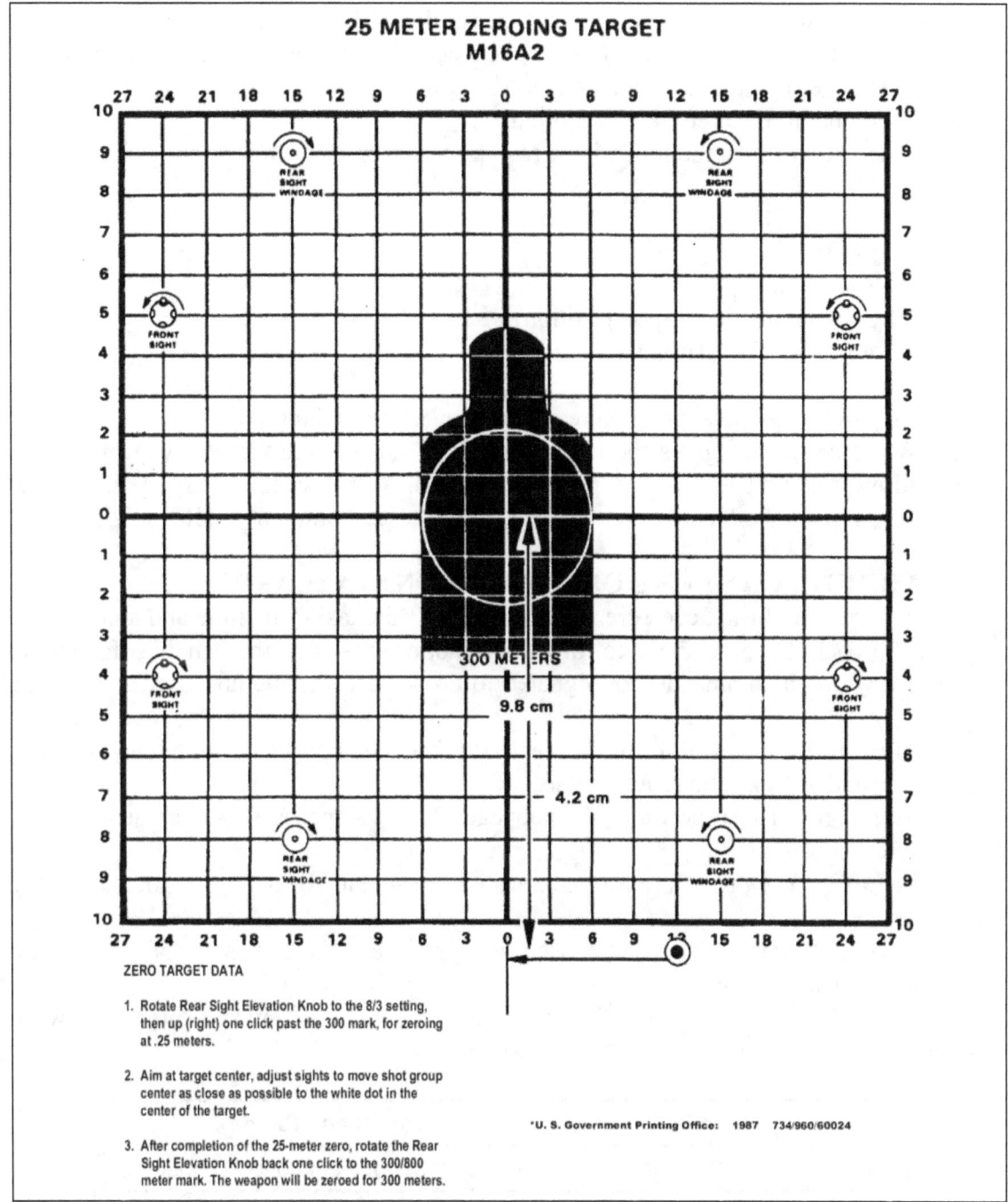

Figure 5-25. Adjustment of rounds.

5-15. NIGHT RECORD FIRE

Night or limited visibility firing trains grenadiers to apply the fundamentals of grenade launcher marksmanship while using the AN/PVS-4 nightsight. This training increases the grenadiers' confidence. Each grenadier learns to zero the M203 to the AN/PVS-4 on the 25-meter range and then fires at one area target on the M203 grenade launcher range. Before night firing, grenadiers receive instruction in its objectives, fundamentals, fire commands, and targets. The unit is organized in firing orders, each consisting of a grenadier and assistant, based on the range constraints. The assistant performs his duties in a manner similar to day record fire. Night record fire consists of one task: station 3, task 6, mid-range fighting position, area target, night.

    a. Load one of the three rounds allotted.

    b. When you receive the following fire command, repeat each element as it is given:

> GRENADIER
> FRONT
> 3 ROUNDS
> 200 (automatic weapon position)
> AT MY COMMAND

    c. Acquire the proper sight picture and announce UP to the grader.

    d. When the grader gives the command FIRE, engage the target given in the fire command until you hit it. Fire any remaining rounds at the second target. You need no other fire command. For each round you fire, your assistant announces HIT or MISS.

5-16. NIGHT RECORD FIRE QUALIFICATION STANDARDS

Before qualification firing, each grenadier must know the tasks, the time and ammunition required for each, the procedures to follow if a stoppage occurs, the penalties for failure to stop firing when commanded or signaled to do so, and the method used for scoring targets.

    a. **Time and Ammunition**. Firing Table II (Table 5-2) provides the night firing task and its time and ammunition requirements.

    b. **Stoppages**. The procedure for stoppages is the same as for other qualification firing exercises.

    c. **Penalties**. The procedure for penalties is the same as for other qualification firing exercises.

    d. **Target Scoring**. The target scoring procedure is the same as for other qualification firing exercises.

    e. **Conditions**. Night record fire trains the grenadier to engage targets between 150 and 250 meters under ideal moonlight conditions.

Time	Rounds	Type	Target and Range
2 minutes	3	HE	Automatic weapon at 200 to 250 meters.

Table 5-2. Firing Table II, night firing qualification.

CHAPTER 6
COMBAT TECHNIQUES OF FIRE

Grenadiers must be trained in the standard methods of applying fire with a grenade launcher. A unit's grenadier program develops well-trained grenadiers who can survive and win on the battlefield. This chapter provides guidance on combat techniques, which include advanced gunnery, fire control methods, and application of fire.

Section I. ADVANCED GUNNERY

Advanced gunnery techniques reinforce basic gunnery and teach the grenadier how and when to use these basics in combat situations. Training advanced gunnery differs slightly from training basic gunnery. This section discusses in detail how to train characteristics of fire, classes of fire, range estimation, and fire commands. It also discusses the easiest and quickest means of applying firing techniques and delivering fire with the M203 grenade launcher.

6-1. CHARACTERISTICS OF FIRE

The characteristics of fire discussed in this section are defined as follows:

a. **Trajectory**. This is the curve described in space by the fired round as it travels to its target. The trajectory rises as the sights are elevated.

b. **Line of Sight**. This is an imaginary line from the gun to the target, as seen through properly adjusted sights.

c. **Ordinate**. This is the vertical distance at any point between the trajectory and the line of sight.

d. **Maximum Ordinate**. This is the greatest vertical distance between the trajectory and the line of sight; it occurs at the highest point of the trajectory.

e. **Danger Space**. This is the area where the round impact or the shrapnel from the round impact injures personnel or destroys the target.

f. **Dead Space**. This is the area(s) where personnel or targets are safe from direct-fire weapons. Ditches, depressions, and ravines are examples of dead spaces.

6-2. CLASSES OF FIRE

Fire distribution is classified three ways:

a. **With Respect to the Ground**. For the M203 grenade launcher, this class of fire refers only to plunging fire. Plunging fire occurs when firing at long ranges, from high ground to low ground, into abruptly rising ground, or across uneven terrain, resulting in a loss of grazing fire at any point along the trajectory. For example, 40-mm grenades fired from the top of a hill follow an arcing trajectory and land in the valley. Figure 6-1 on page 6-2 shows an example of plunging fire.

b. **With Respect to the Target**. This includes four ways to distribute fire (Figure 6-2, page 6-3):

(1) *Frontal*. Frontal fire is directed against a target's front, with the target facing or moving toward the firing position.

(2) *Flanking*. Flanking fire is directed against the target's flank.

(3) *Oblique*. Oblique fire is directed against a target moving or facing at an angle rather than directly toward or perpendicular to the gun.

(4) *Enfilade*. Enfilade fire is directed along the length of a target and may be frontal or flanking, depending on which way the target is facing.

Figure 6-1. Plunging fire.

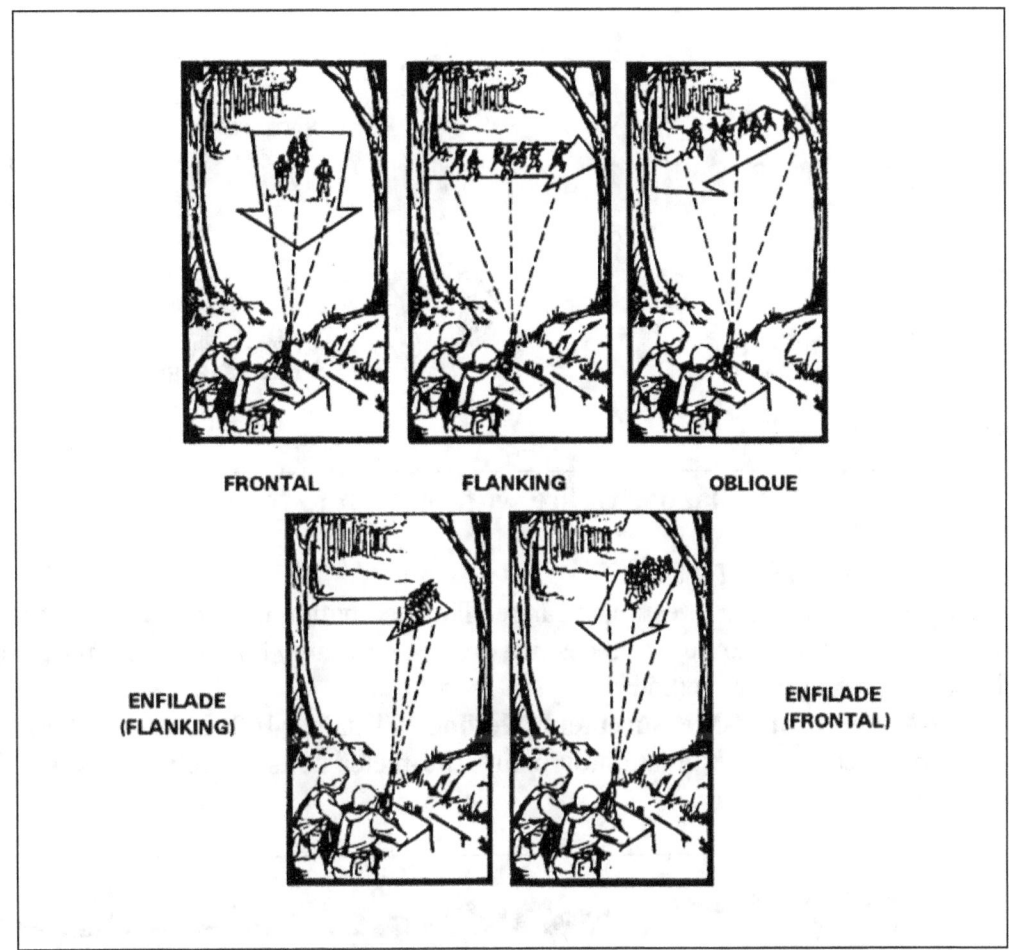

Figure 6-2. Classes of fire with respect to the target.

c. **With Respect to the Weapon**. This also includes four ways to distribute fire (Figure 6-3, page 6-4):

(1) *Rapid Fire Point*. Distribute fire against a target with one aim point.

(2) *Rapid Fire Right or Left*. Distribute fire right to left or left to right without changing range. Use this against frontal or flanking targets.

(3) *Rapid Fire Searching*. Distribute fire against a deep target changing elevation but not direction. Use this fire against enfilade targets.

(4) *Rapid Fire Right or Left and Searching*. Distribute fire against a target with depth and width changing elevation and direction. Use this fire against an oblique target.

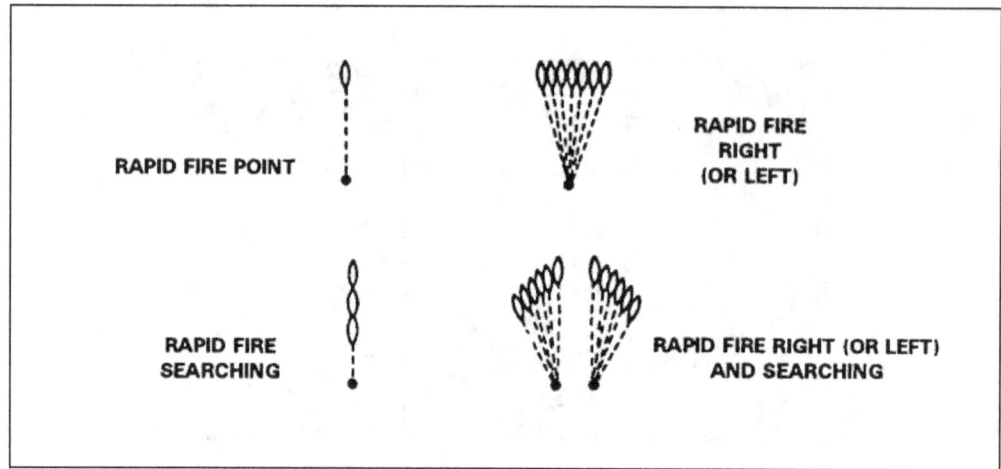

Figure 6-3. Classes of fire with respect to the weapon.

6-3. RANGE ESTIMATION

The grenadier must be able to estimate range. This estimation enables him to hit targets with the first round and to adjust and shift fire if necessary. He often estimates range visually, using one of three methods:

a. **100-Meter Unit-of-Measurement Method**. Visualize 100 meters on the ground (this takes practice). Then estimate how many 100-meter units lie between you and the target (Figure 6-4).

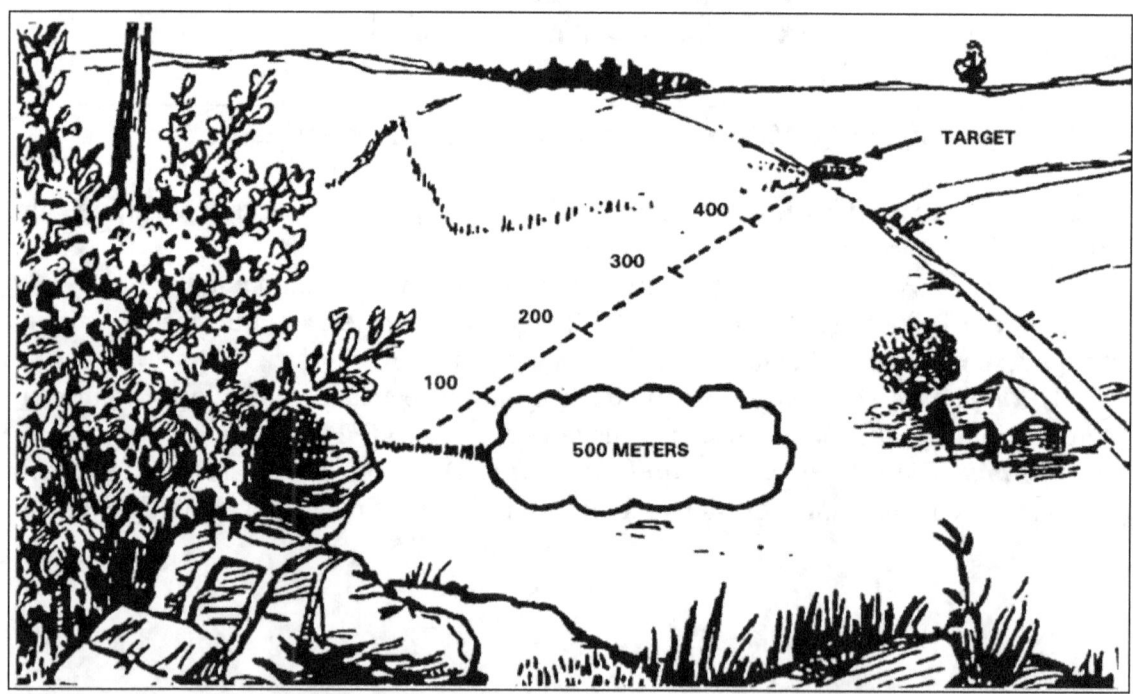

Figure 6-4. Application of the 100-meter unit-of-measurement method.

b. **Appearance-of-Objects Method**. Memorize the sizes and shapes of familiar objects as they appear at different ranges. Remember to consider the factors that affect the appearance of objects (Table 6-1).

Factors that Affect Range Estimation	Factors that Cause Underestimation of Range	Factors that Cause Overestimation of Range
Target detail, outline clarity	Target is mostly visible, and its outline is clear.	Target is only somewhat visible or is seen as small relative to its surroundings.
Nature of terrain or position of observer.	Target is located across a depression that is mostly hidden from view.	Target is located across a depression that is visible.
	Target is located at a ground level below that of the observer.	Target is located at a ground level above that of the observer.
	Target is located down a straight, open road or along a railroad.	Target is located where vision is narrowly confined, such as in streets, draws, or forest trails.
		Target is located across uniform surfaces like water, snow, desert, or fields of grain.
Light and atmosphere	Target is brightly lit, or the sun is shining from behind the observer.	Target is poorly lit, as at dawn or dusk or in rain, snow, or fog, or is obscure because the sun is in the eyes of the observer.
	Target contrasts sharply with the background or is silhouetted due to its size, shape, or color.	Target blends into the background or terrain.
		Target is visible in the clear air of high altitudes.

Table 6-1. Factors that affect visual range estimation.

c. **AN/PVS-4 Method.** Using a target six feet tall, such as a soldier--

(1) Look through the reticle, place the base of the target (or the soldier's feet) on the horizontal line, and try to match the target's height to one of the vertical lines. The number under the line is the distance to the target in hundreds of meters. (For example, the distance to the soldier shown in A, Figure 6-5 on page 6-6 is 400 meters.)

(2) If the soldier is too tall to match to the top half of a vertical line, then match his height to a whole vertical line. Halve the number under the line to obtain the distance to him in hundreds of meters. (For example, the distance to the soldier shown in B, Figure 6-5 on page 6-6 is 200 meters.)

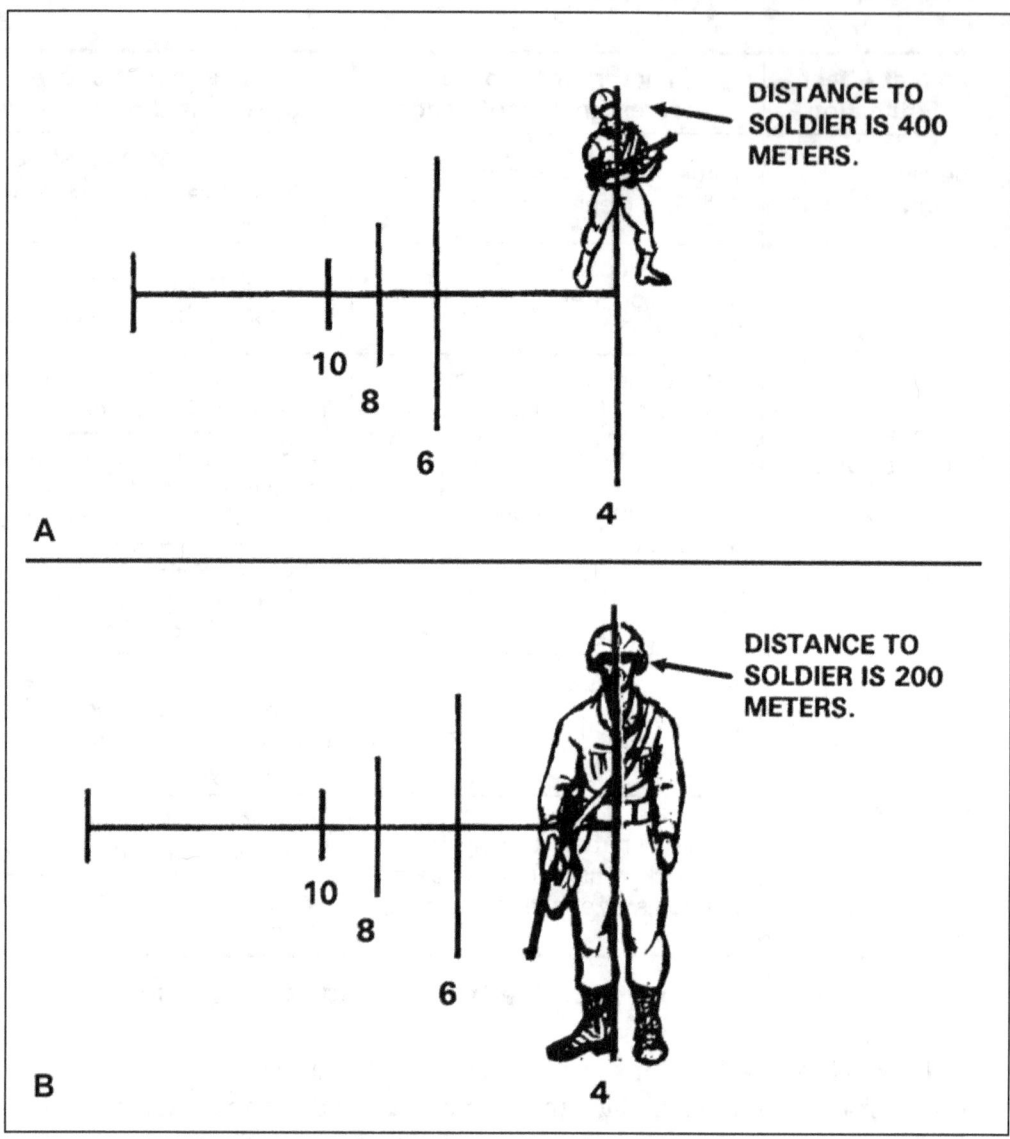

Figure 6-5. Range estimation using the AN/PVS-4 nightsight.

6-4. PREDETERMINED FIRES

Predetermined fires are used to cover such target areas as dead spaces and likely enemy avenues of approach and assault positions. Each squad leader prepares a sector sketch to help in planning the defense and controlling fire (Figure 6-6).

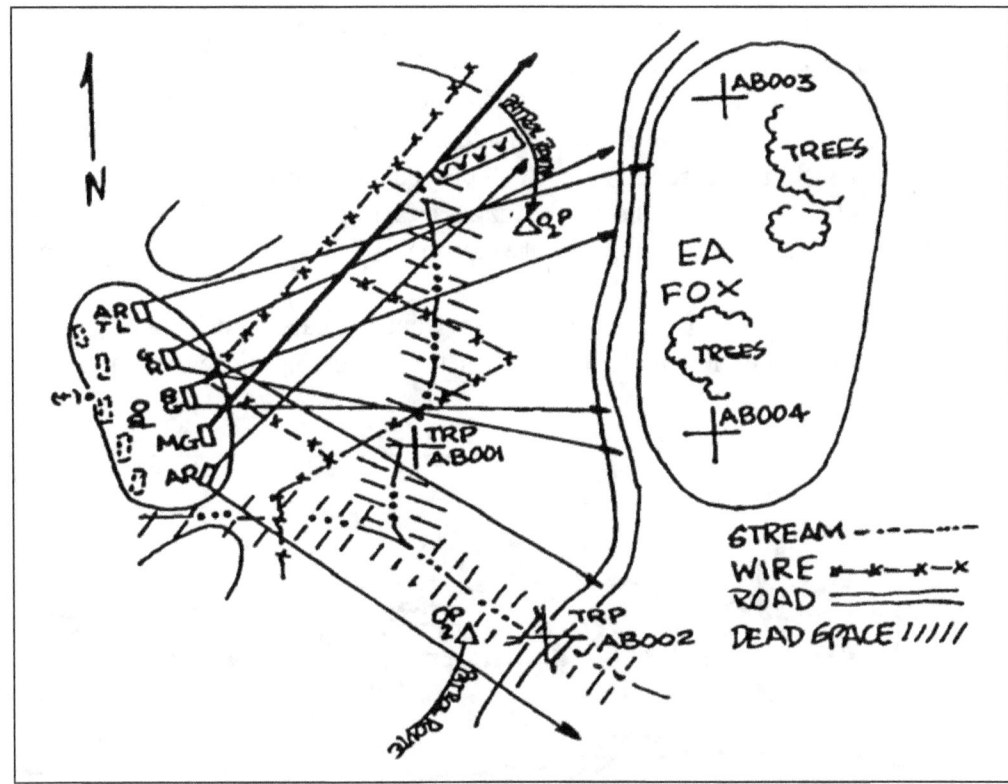

Figure 6-6. Example squad sector sketch.

a. **Determining Dead Space**. The extent of a dead space and the amount of grazing fire required to cover it may be determined by two methods:

(1) The first method requires the grenadier to lay the grenade launcher for elevation and direction and to clear the weapon. A member of the squad then walks along the direction line toward the target while the grenadier looks through his rifle sights. Dead space exists wherever the soldier's waist (midsection) falls below the grenadier's line of aim. The grenadier uses arm-and-hand signals to control the walking soldier. This method gives the grenadier an accurate indication of the location and depth of the dead space.

(2) The second method requires the grenadier to observe the flight of tracer ammunition from a position behind and to the flank of the weapon.

b. **Calling for Fire**. Predetermined targets, including the final protective line (FPL) or principal direction of fire (PDF), are engaged on order or IAW SOP. The signal used to call for these fires is normally stated in the defense order. Fires on predetermined targets may be controlled by arm-and-hand signals, voice commands, or pyrotechnic devices.

6-5. TYPES OF TARGETS

Targets for grenadiers in combat are most likely to be enemy troops. Personnel targets have width and depth; different troop formations require different classes of fire distribution. The fire must thoroughly cover the area where the enemy is known or suspected to be, and the targets may be easy or hard to find.

a. **Point Targets**. These are targets--such as enemy bunkers, windows, weapons emplacements, light-skinned vehicles, and troops--that have a single aiming point. The maximum effective range for point targets is 150 meters.

b. **Area Targets**. These may have considerable width and depth and may require extensive right or left and searching fire. A deployed platoon is one example of an area target. The grenadier must know how to engage area targets regardless of their sizes or shapes. The maximum effective range for area targets is 350 meters. Types of area targets are as follows:

(1) *Linear Targets*. The grenadier sights on what appears to be center of mass. He fires the grenade launcher left and right across the target on successive aiming points (Figure 6-7).

Figure 6-7. Linear targets.

(2) *Deep Targets*. The grenadier first lays on the center of mass of the target. He fires searching fire to the near end and then up to the far end of the target along successive aiming points (Figure 6-8).

Figure 6-8. Deep targets.

(3) *Linear Targets with Depth*. The grenadier lays on the target's center of mass. He then moves the grenade launcher left and right across the target, selecting successive aiming points at different ranges (Figure 6-9).

Figure 6-9. Linear targets with depth.

6-6.   DECONTAMINATION
Leaders must try to reduce the penetration of contaminants and lessen exposure to them. Contaminated material is disposed of in accordance with the SOP.

a.   **Nuclear**. Wipe off the weapon with warm soapy water. Otherwise, use towelettes or rags. (FM 3-5 provides details.)

b.   **Biological**. Use towelettes from the M258A1 kit to wipe off the weapon. If these are not available, wash with soap and water.

c.   **Chemical**. Use soap and water or towelettes as for biological contamination.

Section II. FIRE CONTROL
Fire control includes all leader and soldier actions in planning, preparing, and applying fire on a target. The leader selects and designates targets, indicating their width and depth or, in the case of targets that are hard to identify, designates the distance from a reference point to the target's center of mass (Figure 6-10, page 6-10). He also designates the midpoint, flanks, or ends of a target unless these locations are obvious to the grenadiers. The grenadiers open fire when ready, adjust and regulate the rate of fire, and shift from one target to another. They cease fire only when the target is neutralized or the leader signals to cease fire.

Figure 6-10. Use of a reference point to identify a target.

6-7. METHODS OF FIRE CONTROL

The noise and confusion of battle may limit the methods of fire control used, so the leader must select the method(s) that will best accomplish the mission.

a. **Oral Commands**. The primary method of fire control is the oral fire command. This method is effective unless noise or distance prevents the grenadier from hearing the leader.

b. **Arm-and-Hand Signals**. This method of fire control is effective only if the grenadiers know the standard arm-and-hand signals and can see the leader. The leader gets the grenadier's attention, then points to the target. When the grenadier returns the "ready" signal, the leader commands the grenadier to fire.

c. **Prearranged Signals**. This method of fire control can include visual or sound signals such as those that can be produced by a whistle, pyrotechnics, or casualty-producing device. The SOP must define the signals to be used, and all squad members must understand them. If the leader wants to shift fire at a certain time, he gives a prearranged signal such as smoke or pyrotechnics. When they see this signal, grenadiers shift their fire to a prearranged point.

d. **Personal Contact**. This method of fire control is the one most frequently used by leaders of small units. Many situations require the leader to move to individual soldiers to issue orders. If so, he must use cover and concealment to avoid disclosing their positions. Once there, he gets the grenadier's attention, points out the new target, and commands FIRE.

e. **Standing Operating Procedure**. This method of fire control refers to actions executed without command. The SOP defines these actions and the events that initiate them. Using an SOP simplifies the leader's job of fire control.

f. **Range Cards**. This method of fire control requires the leader to ensure all range cards are current and accurate. He designates dead spaces, specific targets, no-fire zones, and restricted fire areas. The key to this method is the disciplined grenadier who pays attention to detail and can understand the areas the squad leader wants covered by fire. Figure 6-11 shows an example of an M203 range card.

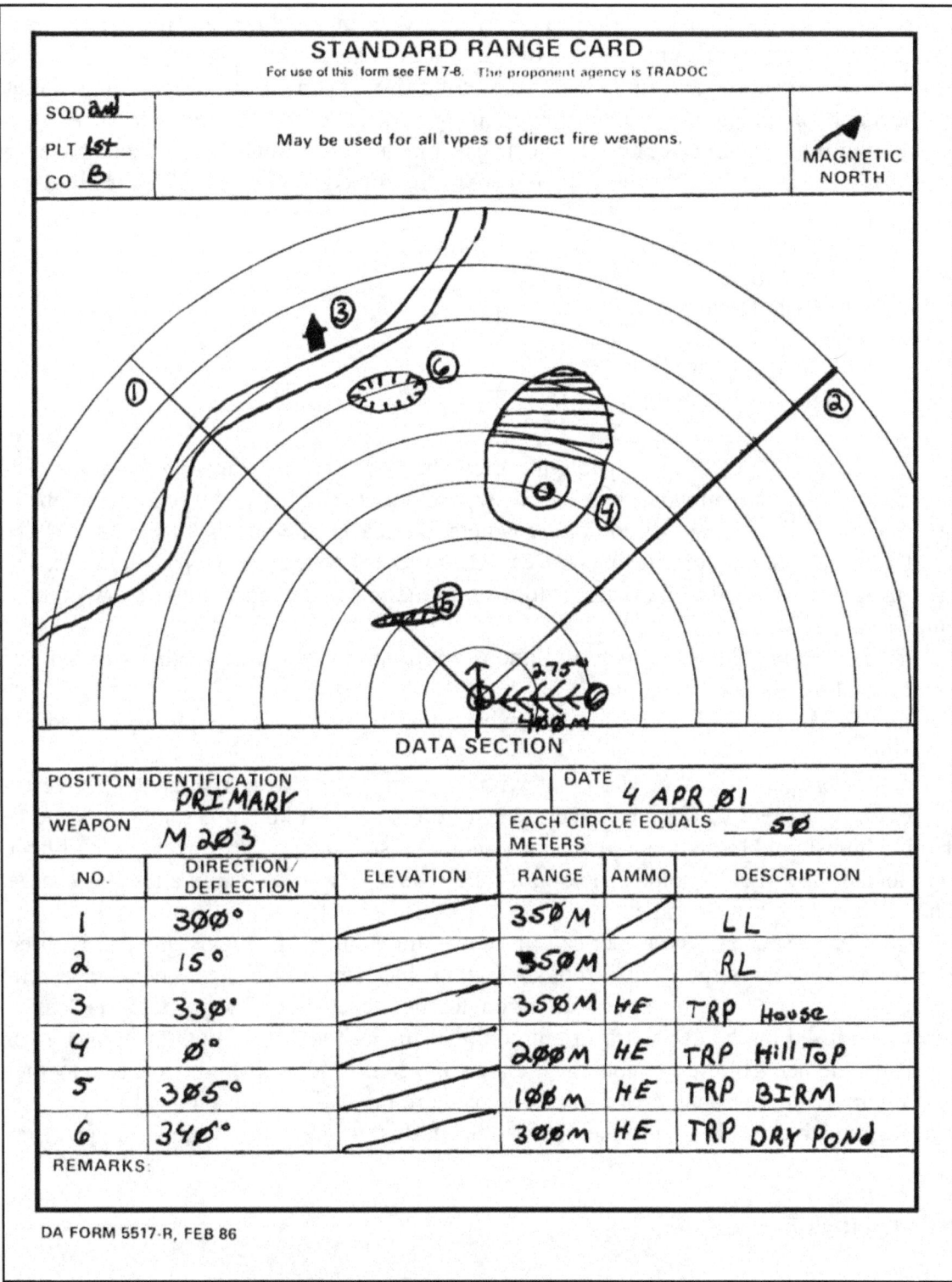

Figure 6-11. Example of an M203 range card.

6-8. FIRE COMMANDS

Leaders give fire commands to get effective fire on a target quickly and without confusion. When the leader decides to engage a target that is not obvious to the grenadier, he must give the grenadier enough information to effectively engage the target.

After he alerts the grenadier, the leader must give a target direction, description, and range; then he must name the method of fire and give the command to fire. Leaders may give initial and subsequent fire commands: initial fire commands initiate fire on a target; subsequent commands adjust, interrupt, or change the rate of fire or terminate the alert.

a. **Initial Fire Commands**. Initial fire commands for grenade launchers have six elements. The grenadiers repeat each element of the fire command as the leader gives it:

    ALERT
    DIRECTION
    DESCRIPTION
    RANGE
    METHOD OF FIRE
    COMMAND TO OPEN FIRE

(1) *Alert*. This element prepares the grenadiers to receive further instructions. The leader may alert both grenadiers in the squad, but only fire one of them (command one of them to fire). To alert and fire both grenadiers, the leader announces GRENADIER. To alert both but fire only one, he announces GRENADIER NUMBER ONE (or TWO). The nonfiring grenadier lays on the target to take up the mission in case the primary grenade launcher malfunctions.

(2) *Direction*. The leader may use one or more of the following methods to indicate the general direction to the target:

(a) *Speaking*. The leader can state where the target is relative to the grenadier's position.

(b) *Pointing*. The leader can point with his arm or aim with a weapon to give the direction to a small or obscure target. When he points with his arm, someone standing behind him should be able to look over his shoulder, sight along his arm and index finger, and locate the target. A soldier looking through the sights of a weapon aimed at a target should be able to see the target.

(c) *Firing Tracers*. The leader can fire tracer ammunition to quickly and surely direct the grenadier to a target that is not clearly visible. He should first give the general direction to draw the grenadier's attention to the target area. To prevent the loss of surprise caused by the use of tracer ammunition, the leader fires only after he has given all of the elements of the fire command except the command to fire. The leader may then fire his individual weapon or may fire one or more bursts from a machine gun. Because tracer fire is the last element of the fire command, it is the grenadier's signal to open fire.

    GRENADIER
    FRONT
    300
    WATCH MY TRACER(S)

(d) *Using Reference Points*. The leader may use easy-to-recognize reference points to direct the grenadier to an obscure target. The leader uses the word "reference" before he describes the terrain feature used to designate the target. He does this to avoid confusion. He should also give the general direction to the reference point. (The reference might be a shift from a known point.) All leaders and grenadiers must know terrain features and the terminology used to describe them (FM 21-26).

GRENADIER NUMBER ONE
FRONT
REFERENCE: LONE PINE TREE   (reference point)

GRENADIER NUMBER ONE
FRONT
REFERENCE: CROSSROADS RIGHT 200   (shift from a known point)

(3) ***Description***. Unless the target is obvious, the leader may describe the target briefly. This enables the grenadiers to picture the type of target so they can properly apply their fire.

(4) ***Range***. The leader estimates the range and announces it to the nearest hundred meters but, because the meter is the standard unit range measurement, he omits the word "meters."

GRENADIER
FRONT
REFERENCE: BARN RIGHT 100
TARGET--TROOPS IN THE OPEN   (description)
300   (range in meters)

(5) ***Method of Fire***. The leader announces the class of fire with respect to the weapon and, unless the fire command requires the grenadier to engage with rapid fire, the number of rounds to use.

GRENADIER
FRONT
REFERENCE: SHIFT FROM MACHINE GUN BUNKER RIGHT 200
TARGET--TROOPS IN THE OPEN
300
RAPID FIRE RIGHT AND SEARCH   (class of fire with respect to weapon)

(6) ***Command to Open Fire***. The leader may preface the command to commence firing with AT MY COMMAND or AT MY SIGNAL. He withholds fire this way to surprise the enemy or to allow both grenadiers to open fire at the same time. After both grenadiers respond READY, the leader commands FIRE at his discretion. If the leader wants immediate fire, he simply commands FIRE without pausing, and the grenadiers fire as soon as they are ready.

```
GRENADIER
FRONT
TROOPS IN THE OPEN
300
AT MY COMMAND or                    (Leader pauses until grenadiers are
   AT MY SIGNAL                      ready and fire is desired)
FIRE (or prearranged signal)
```

b. **Subsequent Fire Commands**. The leader issues subsequent fire commands to adjust direction and elevation, to change the number of rounds to fire after a fire mission is in progress, to interrupt fires, or to terminate the alert. If the grenadier engages a target incorrectly, the leader promptly corrects his fire by announcing or signaling desired changes. The grenadier corrects and resumes firing without further command. The leader adjusts direction first--for example, RIGHT 50 or LEFT 100. He adjusts elevation second--for example, ADD FIVE ZERO or DROP FIVE ZERO. Third, he adjusts the number of rounds. He interrupts fire by signaling or announcing CEASE FIRE or terminates the alert by signaling or announcing CEASE FIRE, END OF MISSION.

c. **Doubtful Elements and Corrections**. The grenadier repeats doubtful elements so the leader will repeat the element--for example, if the range to the target was unclear or inaccurate, the grenadier announces SAY AGAIN RANGE, TARGET. The leader then announces THE COMMAND WAS…, repeats the element in question, and continues with the fire command. The leader can also correct fire commands as follows:

(1) *Initial Fire Command*. Announce CORRECTION and then give the corrected element.

```
GRENADIER
RIGHT FRONT
TROOPS IN THE OPEN
400
CORRECTION
300
RAPID FIRE RIGHT
AT MY COMMAND
```

(2) *Subsequent Fire Command*. Correct an error by announcing CORRECTION and repeating the entire subsequent fire command.

```
LEFT FIVE ZERO, ADD FIVE              (subsequent fire command as given)


CORRECTION
LEFT FIVE ZERO, ADD FIVE ZERO         (correction)
```

d. **Abbreviated Fire Commands**. Fire commands need not be complete to be effective. In combat, the leader gives only the elements necessary to place fire on a target quickly and without confusion. During training, he uses all the elements to enable grenadiers to learn how they are used. After grenadiers receive initial training in fire commands, they should learn to react to abbreviated fire commands, which may be given orally or by arm-and-hand signals.

(1) ***Oral Method***. If the leader wants to place the fire of one grenade launcher on an enemy machine gun bunker he has located, he will say—

GRENADIER NUMBER ONE
MACHINE GUN BUNKER
400
FIRE

(2) ***Arm-and-Hand Method***. To control fire when battlefield noise or distance to the grenadier is too great, the leader must use arm-and-hand signals (Figure 6-12, page 6-16). When he wants a specific grenadier to execute an action or movement, he gives a preliminary signal to that grenadier only. The following signals are commonly used by leaders and grenadiers:

(a) *Ready*. The grenadier gives this signal to indicate that he is ready to fire. He raises his hand or arm above his head toward the leader.

(b) *Commence Firing*. The leader gives this signal by bringing his hand (palm down) to the front of his body about waist level, and moving it horizontally in front of his body.

(c) *Move Over or Shift Fire*. The leader gives this signal by raising his hand (on the side toward the new direction) and moving it across his body to the opposite shoulder, palm to the front; then, with his arm and hand extended, he swings his arm in a horizontal arc to point in the new direction. For slight changes in direction, he moves his hand from the latest position to the desired direction of movement.

(d) *Interrupt or Cease Firing*. The leader gives this signal by raising his arm and hand (palm outward) in front of his forehead and bringing it downward sharply.

(e) *Other Signals*. The leader devises other signals to control his weapons. (FM 21-60 provides a detailed description of arm-and-hand signals.)

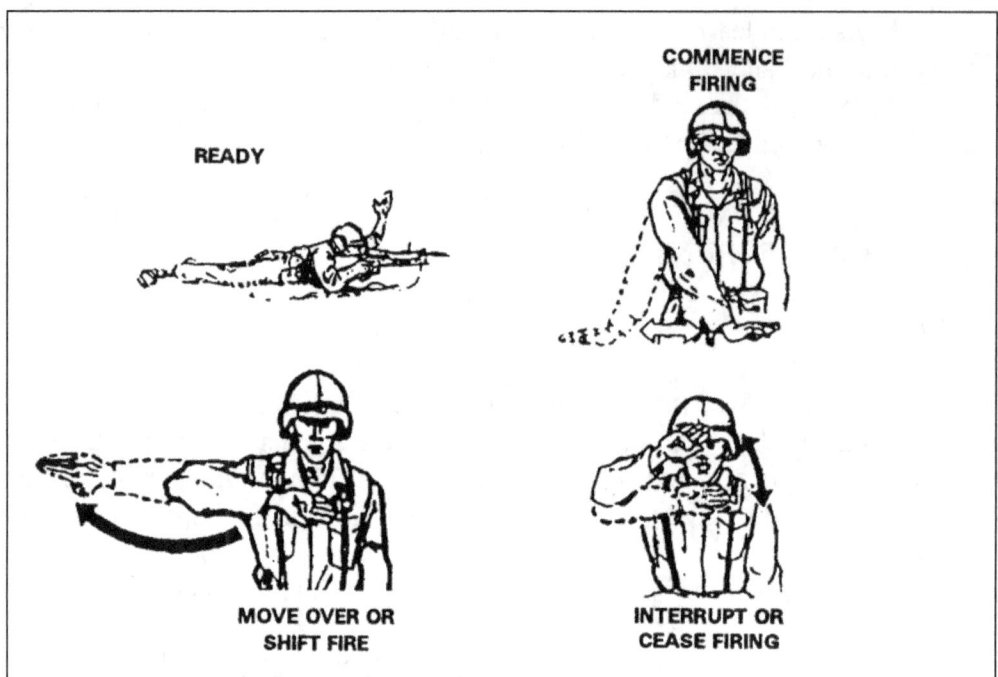

Figure 6-12. Arm-and-hand signals.

Section III. APPLICATION OF FIRE

Application of fire refers to the methods grenadiers must use to completely and effectively cover a target area. They can learn these methods only after they know what types of targets they may find in combat and how to properly distribute and concentrate their fire. Using these methods ensures they can react quickly and properly when they detect or are alerted to various types of targets.

6-9. SUPPRESSIVE FIRE

Grenadiers use suppressive fire to prevent the enemy from seeing, shooting at, or tracking a target. Suppressive fire is direct or indirect fire aimed near enough to the enemy's position to keep him from placing accurate fire on friendly forces.

6-10. OVERWATCH FIRE

Grenadiers use overwatch fire to cover other soldiers' movements. While overwatching, grenadiers perform the following tasks:

    a. They support the platoon by covering dead space.
    b. They learn the platoon's route and its plans.
    c. They select likely enemy positions and observe them continuously.
    d. They determine where to find and how to reach the best grenade launcher position.

6-11. AREA AND POINT FIRE

Grenadiers deliver point fire and area fire in width, depth, or both. To distribute fire properly, they must know where to aim, how to adjust their fire, and where to move the grenade launcher.

a. **Point of Aim**. The grenadier must initially aim, fire, and adjust on a certain point on the target. He must adjust boldly, rapidly, and continuously. In most cases, the enemy leader and the communications section are in the center of the enemy's formation. Because soldiers generally tend to bunch up, the enemy troops may also be located near the center of the enemy formation. Unless a greater threat exists elsewhere, the grenadier should use the center of this concentrated target as the initial aiming point. The leader can use binoculars and help the grenadier adjust fire. For area targets, the grenadier should aim where the bursting radius will achieve its fullest effect.

b. **Direction**. The direction the leader gives depends on the type of target and on whether he wants one or two grenade launchers to engage the target. When a pair engage an area target (not a point target), they divide the target and interlock and distribute their fire over it. After receiving the fire command, the grenadier (or each grenadier) moves his grenade launcher to aim in the designated direction over the target.

6-12. TARGET ENGAGEMENT

The grenadier may be required to engage multiple targets using various combat techniques of fire for area and point targets.

a. A grenadier engages a point target using point fire (also called rapid point fire). If the target moves after the initial round is fired, the grenadier follows the movement of the target to keep fire on it.

b. Because an area target is designated by width and depth, the grenadier engages it by aiming and adjusting on the center of its mass and then moving left or right, searching to either flank to achieve the fullest effect of the bursting radius. When his fire reaches the target's flank, the grenadier reverses direction.

c. The grenadier engages a designated linear target by moving right or left, searching the weapon to distribute fire evenly on the target. He must engage the entire width of a linear target; its midpoint is the point of aim. The grenadier then moves in the opposite direction to cover the rest of the target.

d. The leader announces the range and extent (depth) of a deep target (in meters), using a reference point to designate its center of mass if the target is hard to identify. The grenadier initially aims on the target's midpoint unless another part is more critical. He engages a deep target with searching fire (Figure 6-13, page 6-18). He searches down to an aiming point in front of the near end and back up to an aiming point beyond the far end, always trying to gain the fullest effect of the bursting radius.

e. The leader can fire his rifle to identify a linear target with depth. He should not use the reference point method because showing the angle of this type of target requires at least two reference points. The grenadier engages the midpoint of this target first unless some other part of the target presents a greater threat. He moves left or right and searches to the near flank then back to the far flank (Figure 6-14, page 6-18).

Figure 6-13. Engagement of deep targets.

Figure 6-14. Engagement of linear targets with depth.

6-13. LIMITED VISIBILITY

Limited visibility degrades the grenadiers' ability to detect and identify targets and the leader's ability to control fire. The leader may instruct the grenadiers to fire without command as soon as targets become visible. Grenadiers should engage only targets they can identify unless ordered to do otherwise. Leaders should fire tracer ammunition to help the grenadiers locate and engage targets during limited visibility. The center and flanks of the targets may not be clearly defined; each grenadier must observe his leader's tracers and those from other squad weapons and cover what he believes to be the entire target.

6-14. OVERHEAD FIRE

Grenadiers deliver fire over the heads of friendly soldiers in combat <u>only</u>, and then only when the fire command specifies. Terrain and visibility dictate when they can fire overhead safely. (AR 385-63 summarizes training safety requirements.)

> **WARNING**
> Do not fire overhead fire through trees. Rounds may arm at 14 meters, which is near enough to deflect off nearby trees or structures, causing injury.

CHAPTER 7
TRAIN-THE-TRAINER PROGRAM

This chapter provides information to help the chain of command--the primary trainers--develop an effective train-the-trainer program. The key to successful unit marksmanship training is the knowledge level of small-unit leaders and trainers. Section I discusses the organization of the program, Section II provides the train-the-trainer tasks, and Section III discusses trainer certification.

Section I. ORGANIZATION

An effective unit-level train-the-trainer program reflects the training priorities and interests of the chain of command. The training strategy for the train-the-trainer program is to develop METLs. To do this, the chain of command assesses the overall training program, their own responsibilities, and those of the trainers and coaches.

7-1. OBJECTIVES

The train-the-trainer program has specific objectives. These objectives are to develop in every trainer the confidence, willingness, knowledge, and skills required to consistently train soldiers to use an M203 effectively. The program's aim is for the chain of command to train their trainers and--

- To train soldiers to apply the fundamentals.
- To diagnose and correct marksmanship areas.
- To achieve standards.
- To maintain a constant degree of proficiency.
- To establish a trainer base.

7-2. MISSION-ESSENTIAL TASK LIST

Grenadier proficiency is critical to the squad and platoon. Each commander should develop a METL for both defensive and offensive operations and then organize a training program that devotes adequate time to M203 gunnery. The commander considers the unit's combat mission when he establishes training priorities. This applies to the selected tasks and the conditions under which the tasks are to be performed.

7-3. TRAINER ASSESSMENT

The chain of command identifies the soldiers who have the required knowledge, skills, and motivation in M203 gunnery and trains these soldiers to pass their knowledge on to other soldiers.

a. **Selection**. Potential trainers are selected from the best qualified soldiers. To be trainers, the soldiers must display motivation and know the M203 grenade launcher. They must demonstrate both their proficiency in applying the fundamentals of M203 gunnery and their ability to train professionally. Because knowledgeable trainers are the key to M203 gunnery performance, the commander must maintain high standards for trainer expertise.

b. **Training**. The more time a command invests in training a trainer, the better the result. The chain of command should periodically evaluate trainers and replace any who have lost their desire to accomplish the objectives of the M203 gunnery program. To maintain interest, commanders may promote competitive trainer awards such as "Trainer of the Month."

7-4. ASSISTANT TRAINERS AND CADRE COACHES

Assisting and coaching other soldiers in firing the M203 grenade launcher are important technical jobs. The most valuable soldiers in the M203 gunnery training program are those who are most proficient in and can best transmit their knowledge of M203 gunnery to others. Soldiers who demonstrate consistency as grenadiers should be identified quickly and developed into competent assistant trainers or coaches. Their main responsibility then becomes to teach other soldiers to use the M203 grenade launcher effectively. Training a qualified grenadier to become a successful coach is worth the effort. A less obvious benefit is that such training also develops leadership ability.

a. **Assistant Trainers**. Assistant trainers maintain discipline on the firing line and constantly enforce compliance with training guidance, range regulations, and safety regulations (Appendix D discusses range safety).

b. **Coaches**. Coaches must know the fundamentals of both accurate firing and coaching. Therefore, each coach must meet the following qualifications:

(1) *Knowledge*. A coach must know this manual and must be able to answer any questions on the subject of M203 gunnery accurately. He must develop his ability to observe soldiers' actions in detail and offer quick correction and sound guidance.

(2) *Patience*. A coach will encounter many types of soldiers who try his patience. This includes dull, know-it-all, uncooperative, and aggressive ones. He must handle each one patiently. Through demonstration and repetition, coaches can train soldiers to be proficient M203 grenadiers.

(3) *Understanding*. Because training new grenadiers is stressful to both students and the coach, a coach needs a good "firing line manner." Soldiers may be sensitive to abruptness, impatience, or lack of sympathy. If so, they will react immediately and unfavorably to any evidence of these from the coach.

(4) *Consideration*. Most soldiers, even those who do not fire well, enjoy firing and start out with a positive interest in their performance on the range. A coach who is considerate of soldiers' feelings from the beginning, and who encourages them throughout their training, will find coaching a pleasant and rewarding duty.

(5) *Respect*. Because a coach must be an expert grenadier, he should receive the same respect as the primary trainer. A coach retains that respect by showing that he knows the subject quietly and with dignity.

(6) *Alertness*. The most capable soldier may forget a vital point from his training in the excitement of range firing. The coach must be alert for this possibility and patiently correct the grenadier when it occurs. The coach constantly encourages and motivates the grenadier by providing positive feedback on all progress.

(7) *Helpful Attitude*. A combative attitude is no more effective on the range than in other types of training.

(8) *Encouragement*. The coach can encourage soldiers by convincing them that good firing is no mystery. The weapon and ammunition are mechanically developed for

accuracy: poor scores are usually due to lack of maintenance, knowledge, or practice on the part of the grenadier. The coach imparts his knowledge and helps the soldiers gain the practical experience needed.

7-5. COMMAND BENEFITS

The chain of command must demonstrate active and aggressive leadership in order to establish and maintain a perpetual base of trainer expertise. Unit esprit de corps increases when trainers want to improve and demonstrate they are the best. The goal of a progressive train-the-trainer program is to achieve a high state of combat readiness.

7-6. PROGRAM PHASES

The phases of the train-the-trainer program include preliminary marksmanship training, basic gunnery, and advanced gunnery. To ensure soldiers know gunnery fundamentals before they have to engage real combat targets, trainers must allow the soldiers to advance through the phases of M203 gunnery training only after satisfying certain prerequisites. The trainers' objectives at each phase are to teach soldiers to obtain an accurate initial round impact, to adjust fire, and to do both quickly. The train-the-trainer program provides the trainer with the technical, organizational, and teaching skills necessary to train M203 gunnery tasks.

Section II. TRAINING TASKS

This section provides guidance to help trainers train the M203 grenade launcher effectively. It is divided into phases and provides the tasks, organization, equipment needed, and training sequence for each phase.

7-7. PHASE I, PRELIMINARY MARKSMANSHIP INSTRUCTION

This paragraph discusses how trainers teach soldiers to maintain their assigned weapons.

Task 1. Disassemble the M203 grenade launcher.

Equipment Needed. The trainer displays the M203 on a table. This allows students to see the parts as he removes them. He can use nomenclature charts or mats to help explain the mechanics and to help the grenadiers learn the names of parts.

Class Organization. Ideally, the trainer assigns one assistant trainer and one grenade launcher to each group; otherwise, the trainer may have assistant trainers supervise more than one assigned group.

Sequence of Training. The trainer presents a brief history of the grenade launcher. He discusses the combat role and missions of the weapon and the purpose, scope, and importance of this training. He briefly describes the operation of the weapon and provides general data and exterior nomenclature of the grenade launcher. Assistant trainers should disassemble the grenade launcher as the trainer explains the procedures. Then the grenadiers practice disassembling the weapon until they can demonstrate their skill to an assistant trainer. This training approach encourages practice during free time, which develops individual skills and initiative. The trainer stresses that this task must be performed carefully to avoid damaging parts of the grenade launcher.

Task 2. Inspect the M203 grenade launcher.

Equipment Needed. This is the same as for Task 1, plus one dummy round per weapon.

Class Organization. This is the same as for Task 1.

Sequence of Training. The trainer emphasizes meticulous cleaning, lubrication, inspection, and preventive maintenance to ensure smooth weapon performance. He discusses how important smoothly functioning weapons are to a unit in combat conditions, which are the final test of the weapon maintenance program. He continues training to increase the grenadier's knowledge of M203 nomenclature and skill in disassembling the weapon. He stresses the importance of frequent inspections as a means of ensuring the grenade launcher is properly maintained.

Task 3. Clean the M203 grenade launcher.

Equipment Needed. The trainer needs rags, CLP, one bore-cleaning brush, and one dummy round for each weapon. He should display all of these.

Class Organization. This is the same as for Task 1.

Sequence of Training. This is the same as for Task 2. The trainer discusses the additional care and cleaning required after an NBC attack. He again emphasizes the importance of frequent inspections as a means to ensure proper maintenance.

Task 4. Lubricate the M203 grenade launcher.

Equipment Needed. This is the same as for Task 2.

Class Organization. This is the same as for Task 1.

Sequence of Training. This is the same as for Tasks 2 and 3.

Task 5. Assemble the M203 grenade launcher.

Equipment Needed. This is the same as for Task 1.

Class Organization. This is the same as for Task 1.

Sequence of Training. This is the same as for Task 1.

Task 6. Explain the operation of the M203 grenade launcher.

Equipment Needed. Each two-soldier group requires one M203 grenade launcher, a dummy round, and a cleaning rod, which should be placed on a table before training begins.

Class Organization. This is the same as for Task 1.

Sequence of Training. The trainer explains and demonstrates the proper method of loading, unloading, and clearing the grenade launcher, stressing safety throughout.

Task 7. Explain the functioning of the M203 grenade launcher.

Equipment Needed. Graphic training aids are useful if the class is about the size of a platoon; otherwise, these aids may be made available for study and discussion during breaks. The trainer uses one grenade launcher for each two-soldier group, as in previous mechanical training.

Class Organization. This is the same as for Task 1.

Sequence of Training. The trainer divides functioning into its eight steps--unlocking, cocking, extracting, ejecting, loading, chambering, locking, and firing. Using the grenade launcher assigned to each group, assistant trainers duplicate each demonstration for the benefit of the students (Chapter 2). The students learn how the weapon functions by watching the parts work, rather than by memorizing the text. The trainer tests retention by asking questions about the eight steps.

Task 8. Explain malfunction, stoppage, and immediate action.

Equipment Needed. This is the same as for Task 1.

Class Organization. This is the same as for Task 1.

Sequence of Training. The trainer may use the malfunction and stoppage charts as a guide for presenting training (Tables 4-1 and 4-2). He discusses precise application of the procedures on the charts; then, as grenadiers progress, he shifts his emphasis to speed. Throughout his discussion, he emphasizes safety precautions.

Task 9. Identify types and capabilities of standard 40-mm ammunition.

Equipment Needed. This is the same as for Task 1.

Class Organization. This is the same as for Task 1.

Sequence of Training. The trainer may use the ammunition chart as a guide for presenting training (Figure 3-9). He stresses the importance of knowing ammunition types, their characteristics, and their capabilities. He also stresses why 40-mm ammunition not designed for the M203 grenade launcher must not be used.

7-8. PHASE II, BASIC GUNNERY

This phase is essential to developing the trainer who is to conduct the zeroing and transition day and night record firing for the M203.

Task 1. Conduct day record fire of the M203 on the grenade launcher range.

Equipment Needed. The demonstration crew should have an M203 grenade launcher, a zeroing target, stop watches, a cleaning rod, rags, and CLP. They should also have sound equipment for use during firing.

Class Organization. Preferably, one grenadier, one assistant grenadier, and one assistant trainer should be allotted for each station. Soldiers who are not required on the station or helping operate the range should receive concurrent training.

Sequence of Training. Before the conference and firing demonstration, the trainer briefly reviews range estimation and techniques of adjustment. The grenadiers zero their weapons before training. The station trainers require the grenadiers to be in the correct firing position before letting them fire. The assistant may assist the grenadier in locating the targets, but he is not permitted to aid in range estimation of fire adjustments. At the completion of this exercise, the grenadier and assistant rotate.

Task 2. Conduct night record fire of the M203 on the grenade launcher range.

Equipment Needed. This is the same as for Phase I, Task 2, with the addition of an AN/PVS-4 with an M203 mount or an AN/PVS-7 with aiming stakes.

Class Organization. This is the same as for Phase I, Task 2.

Sequence of Training. This is the same as for Phase I, Task 2.

Section III. TRAINER CERTIFICATION

The trainer certification portion of the train-the-trainer program is designed to sustain training expertise and to develop methods of training. Trainer certification standardizes procedures for certifying M203 gunnery trainers. It also supports the intent of the directives for cadre professional development in TRADOC Regulation 350-6. Trainers' technical expertise must be continuously refreshed, updated, and closely managed.

7-9. TRAINING BASE

Like any organization, the training base has personnel turnover. Additionally, soldiers assigned as M203 trainers have different backgrounds and knowledge of training procedures and methods. Trainer certification is an ongoing process that addresses these variables. M203 trainers must complete the three phases of trainer certification in order and must update their training quarterly. Formal records document each trainer's progress. One of the goals of trainer certification is to help trainers understand the training mission, which helps them support grenadiers.

7-10. CERTIFICATION OUTLINE

Before they can be certified, trainers attend all phases of the program. Then, under the supervision of the chain of command, they conduct the phases. They must demonstrate that they can train soldiers as well as diagnose and correct problem areas. Phases occur in the following sequence:

Phase I, Orientation. During this phase, the new trainer must accomplish the following and obtain certification from the chain of command:

- Attend briefing on the concept of trainer certification.
- Attend briefing on the unit's marksmanship training strategy.
- Review the unit's marksmanship training outlines.
- Review issued reference material.
- Visit training sites and firing ranges.

Phase II, Preliminary Marksmanship Instruction. During this phase, the trainer must demonstrate his mastery of the fundamentals of marksmanship, his ability to diagnose problem areas, and his ability to train others to standards. This phase should be completed within two weeks after Phase I. The following M203 marksmanship fundamentals are reviewed by the chain of command, with the results recorded and maintained on the trainer's progress sheet:

- Characteristics.
- Capabilities.
- Disassembly.
- Cleaning, lubricating, and inspecting.
- Assembly.
- Malfunctions, stoppages, and immediate action.
- Types and capabilities of standard 40-mm ammunition.
- Range estimation.
- Classes of fire.
- Application of fire.

Phases III and IV, Gunnery Training.

Phase III. During this phase, the trainer must demonstrate his ability to set up and conduct firing on the various ranges. He must brief the chain of command to convince them that he can understand the reasons for firing, targetry, and zeroing and scoring procedures. He must also be able to explain the purpose of transition, night, and NBC firing exercises. The results of this interview are recorded and maintained on the trainer's progress sheet.

Phase IV. During this phase, the trainer's knowledge is tested completely. The trainer sets up a range and trains at least one person. If ammunition is available, he conducts a firing exercise. If no ammunition is available, the testing is based on the quality of his training.

APPENDIX A
40-MM GRENADE LAUNCHER, M79

This appendix provides guidance for US Army units to conduct training with the M79 grenade launcher. It discusses the weapon's characteristics, disassembly and assembly procedures, maintenance, sights, operation and function, marksmanship training, firing positions, indirect fire role, and safety precautions.

A-1. DESCRIPTION
The M79 grenade launcher is a single-shot, break-open, breech-loading, shoulder-fired weapon (Figure A-1). It consists of a receiver group, fore-end assembly, barrel group, sight assembly, stock assembly, and sling. A rubber recoil pad is attached to the butt of the stock to absorb some of the recoil.

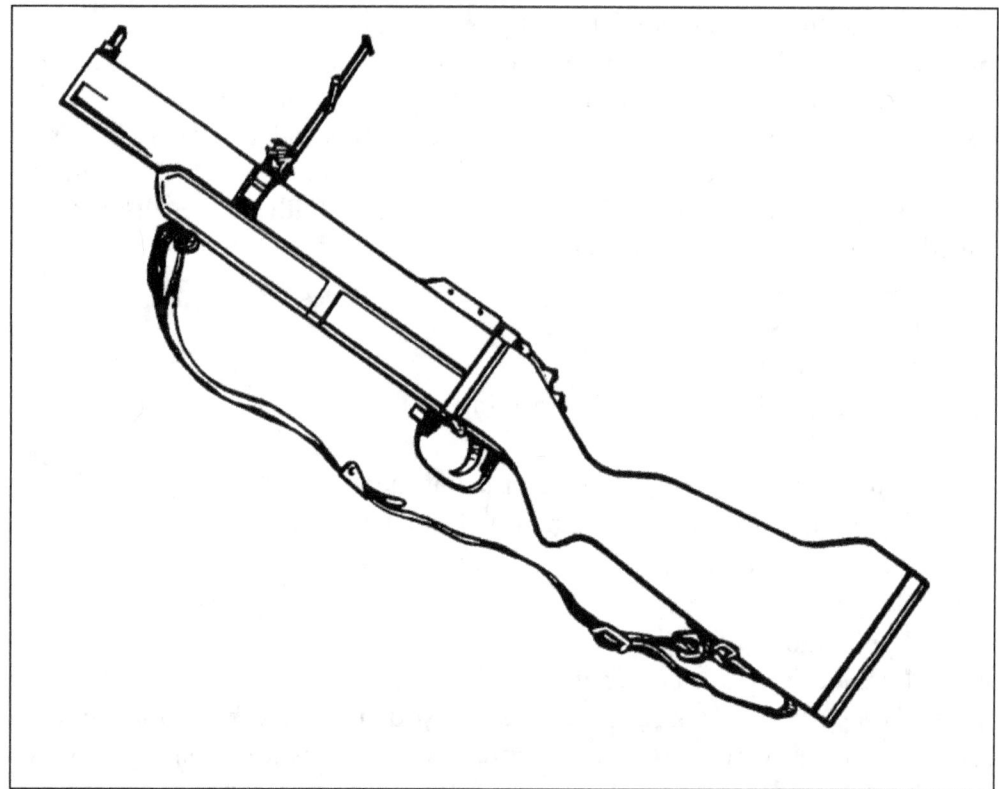

Figure A-1. M79 grenade launcher with rear sight up.

A-2. TECHNICAL DATA
Technical data for the M79 grenade launcher are as follows:

   a. **Weapon**.
      Length:
         Launcher (overall)........................73.70 cm (29 inches)
         Barrel group ....38.10 cm (15 inches)
         Barrel only ....35.60 cm (14 inches)

Weight:
    Unloaded ....2.72 kg (6.0 pounds)
    Loaded...2.95 kg (6.5 pounds)

b. **Ammunition**.
    Caliber...40 mm
    Weight...227 grams (8 ounces)

c. **Operational Characteristics**.
    Action...Break-open, single shot
    Sights:
        Front..Blade-type
        Rear ....:............Folding leaf-type, adjustable
    Chamber pressure..............................17,685 kilopascals (3,000 pounds psi)
    Muzzle velocity..................................76 mps (250 fps)
    Maximum range ....400 meters (1,312 feet)
    Maximum effective range:
        Area target....................................350 meters (1,148 feet)
        Point target...................................150 meters (492 feet)
    Minimum safe firing range:
        Training..130 meters (426 feet)
        Combat...31 meters (102 feet)

A-3.   COMPONENTS

The major components of the 40-mm grenade launcher are shown in Figure A-2. The front and rear sights, the safety, the trigger and trigger guard detent assembly, and the barrel locking latch and lever are shown in Figures A-3 through A-8.

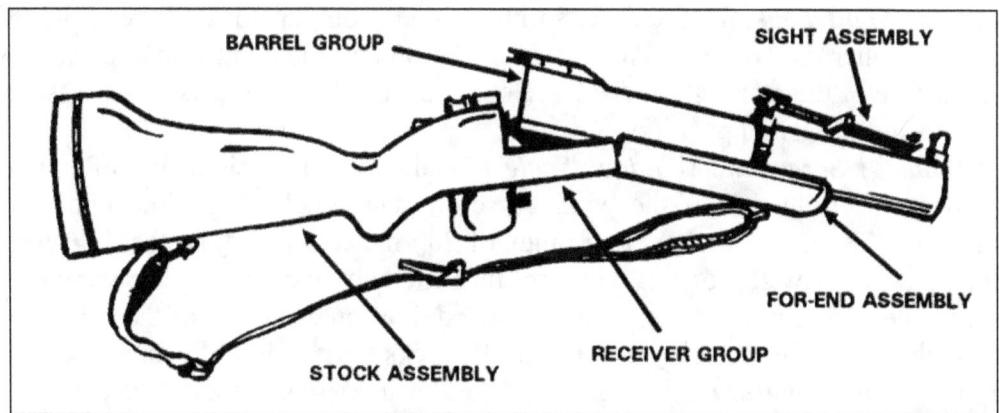

Figure A-2. Relationship of components.

    a. **Rear Sight Assembly**. Figure A-3 shows the adjustable rear sight assembly, which consists of a rear sight lock, a windage screw and scale, an elevation scale and lock screw, a sight carrier and retainer locknut, an elevating screw wheel and elevating screw, and a rear sight frame with fixed leaf sight. To align the rear sight with the front sight, adjust the ladder on the rear sight.

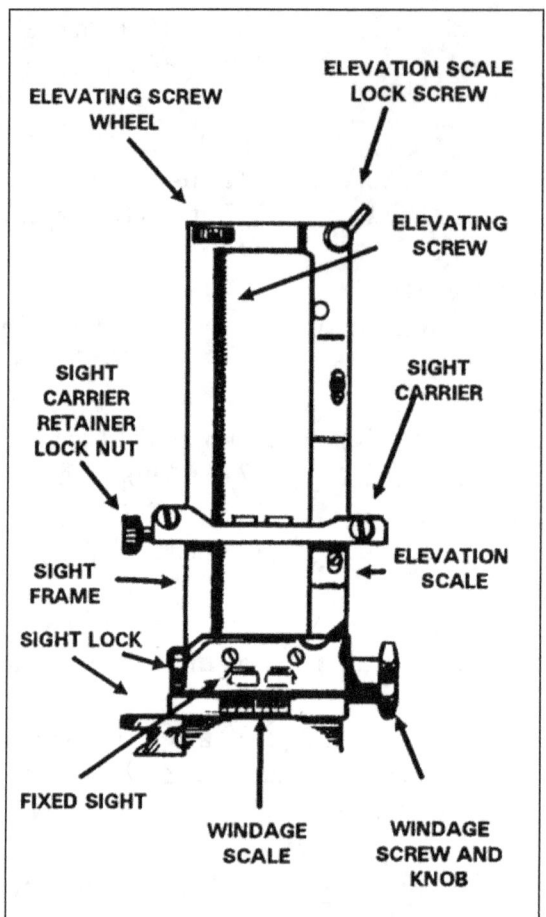

Figure A-3. Rear sight.

(1) ***Rear Sight Lock***. This lock is spring-loaded; you can lock the rear sight frame assembly in either the UP or DOWN position. To unlock the sight frame, push down on the flat surface of the rear sight lock. To relock the sight frame, release the pressure once the frame is in the desired position.

(2) ***Windage Screw and Windage Scale***. To adjust the rear sight for deflection, turn the knob on the right end of the windage screw. One click moves the impact of the grenade about 28 cm (11 inches) at a range of 200 meters. To adjust for right windage, turn the screw clockwise; for left windage, turn it counterclockwise. The windage scale has a zero line in its center and ten equally spaced lines on each side of the zero line. You can move the rear sight assembly as much as 42 clicks right or left of center.

(3) ***Elevation Scale and Lock Screw***. The elevation scale is graduated from 75 to 375 meters in 25-meter increments and numbered at 100, 200, 300, and 375 meters. As you move the rear sight carrier up the adjustable elevation scale, the rear sight cams to the left to compensate for the normal right-hand drift of the projectile. The lock screw holds the elevation scale in position.

(4) ***Sight Carrier Retainer Locknut***. Position and clamp the carrier to the sight frame in the desired position on the elevation scale. Turn the retainer locknut counterclockwise until you can push it inward. The inward pressure unlocks the sight carrier, which allows

you to move it along the elevation scale. To lock the sight carrier in position, release the pressure on the retainer locknut and turn the nut clockwise until it stops.

(5) *Elevating Screw and Screw Wheel*. Use the elevating screw and screw wheel to make fine adjustments in elevation. Turn the wheel clockwise to increase the elevation setting, counterclockwise to decrease it. Turning the screw moves the sight carrier along the elevation scale. One complete turn (one click) moves the impact of the round about 2 1/2 meters at a range of 200 meters.

(6) *Rear Sight Frame with Fixed Sight*. When the rear sight frame is in the DOWN position, use the fixed sight to engage targets up to 100 meters away.

b. **Front Sight**. Figure A-4 shows the stationary front sight, which has a tapered blade and two blade guards.

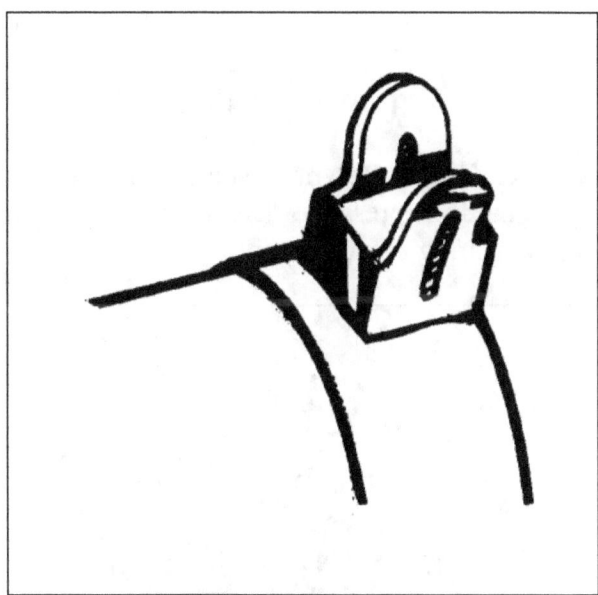

Figure A-4. Front sight.

c. **Safety**. To fire the launcher, ensure the safety is positioned forward (A, Figure A-5) with the letter "F" visible near the rear of the safety. It will not fire if the letter "S" is visible. The safety automatically engages when you unlock the barrel locking latch and open the breech (B, Figure A-5).

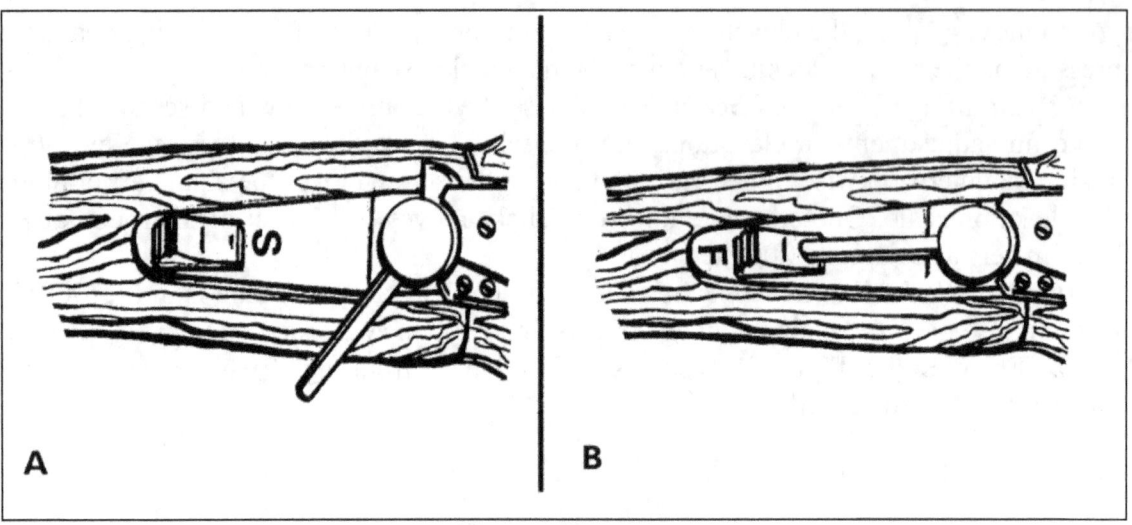

Figure A-5. Safety.

d. **Trigger and Trigger Guard Detent Assembly**. Figure A-6 shows the locations of the trigger and trigger guard. Depress the detent assembly to move the trigger guard right or left or to fire when wearing gloves or mittens.

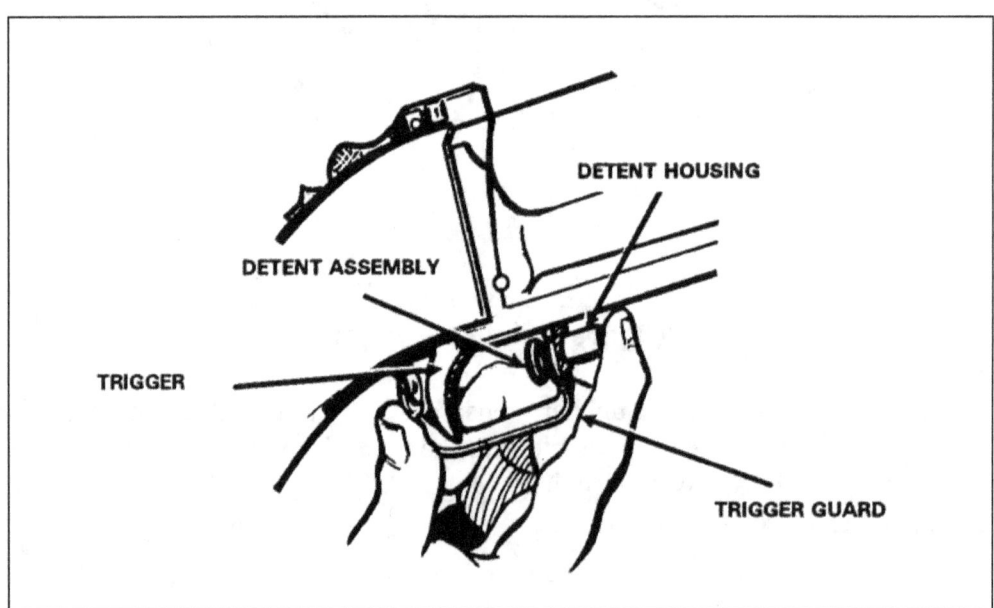

Figure A-6. Position of trigger and trigger guard.

e. **Barrel Locking Latch and Lever**. Figure A-7 on page A-6 shows the barrel locking latch on top of the receiver. This latch locks the barrel and the receiver together. To open (break) the breech end of the barrel, press the latch lever all the way to the right.

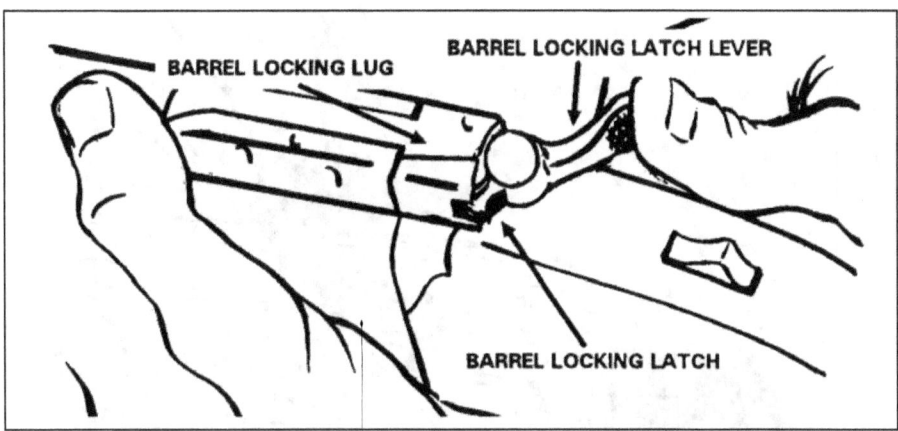

Figure A-7. Operation of the barrel locking latch.

A-4.   AMMUNITION
The M79 grenade launcher uses standard M203 grenade launcher ammunition, which is issued IAW unit SOP.

A-5.   CLEARING PROCEDURE
Clearing the weapon is always the first step in performing maintenance or handling.
    a.   Place the weapon on SAFE.
    b.   Rotate the barrel locking lever fully to the right.
    c.   Open the barrel.
    d.   Inspect the breech to ensure it is clear (no round is present).
    e.   Return the barrel to the firing position.

A-6.   GENERAL DISASSEMBLY
The grenadier places each part he removes on a clean, flat surface (such as a table, shelter half, or disassembly mat) in the order they are removed. This helps in reassembly.

NOTE: Ordnance personnel must disassemble the weapon beyond the level described in this paragraph.

    a.   Remove the sling from the stock.
    b.   Remove the retaining band screw, which passes through the rear of the front sling swivel mount, and pull the fore-end assembly away from the barrel (Figure A-8 and Figure A-9).

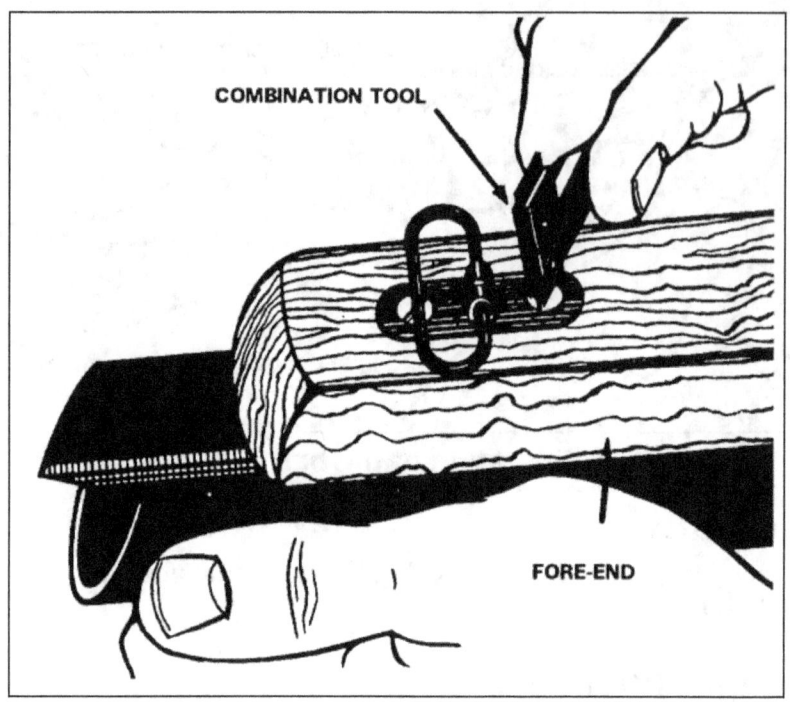

Figure A-8. Removing or installing the retaining band screw.

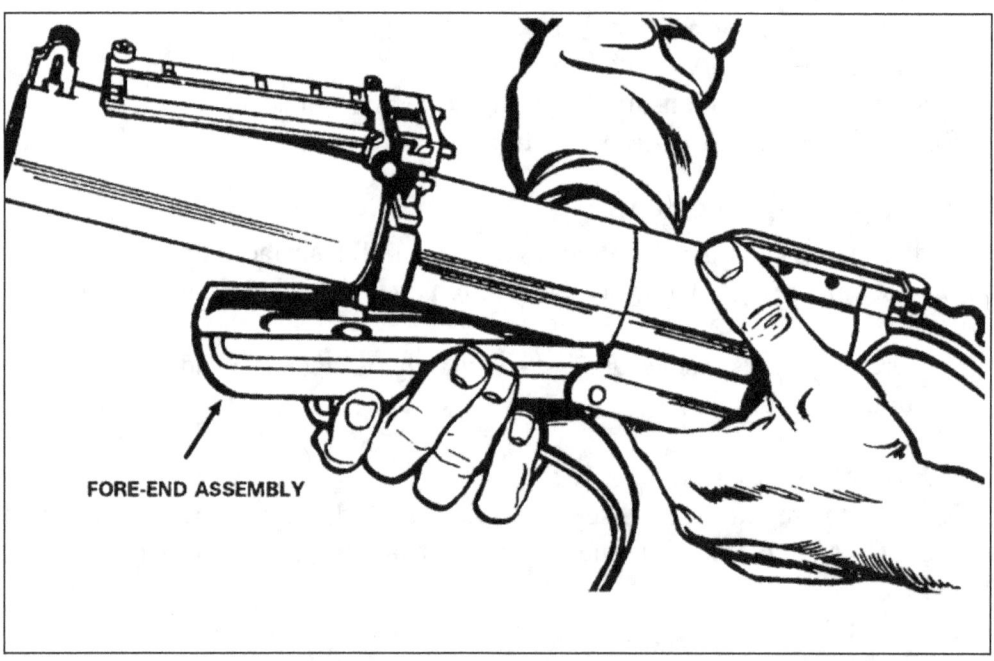

Figure A-9. Removing or installing the fore-end assembly.

    c. Press the barrel locking latch lever to the right and pivot the barrel down until it stops. Slide the barrel off the fulcrum pin and remove it from the receiver (Figure A-10, page A-8). Do not remove the rear sight from the barrel.

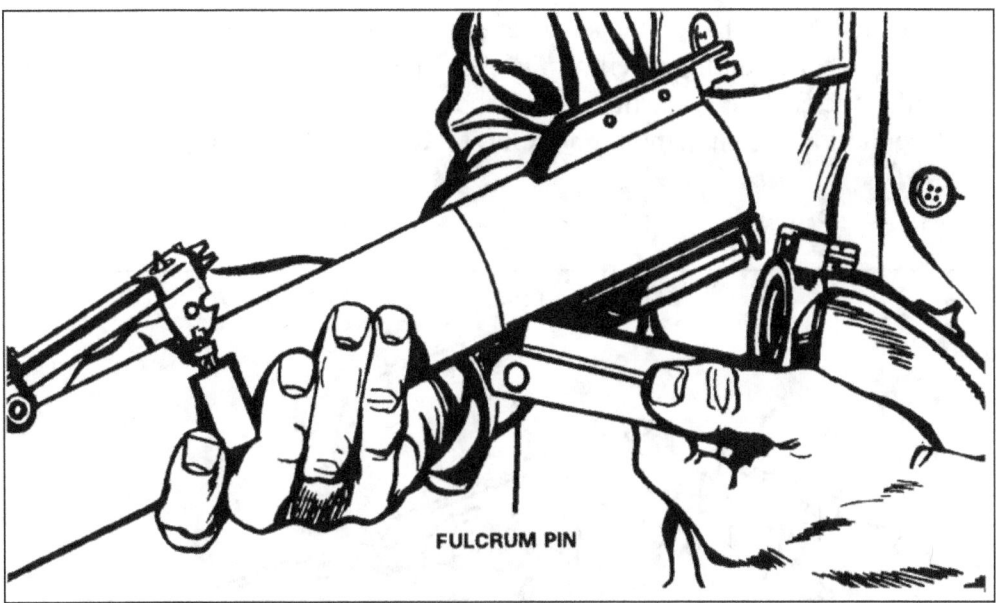

Figure A-10. Removing or installing the barrel group.

d. Remove the stock screw and washers and pull the stock rearward from the receiver (Figure A-11).

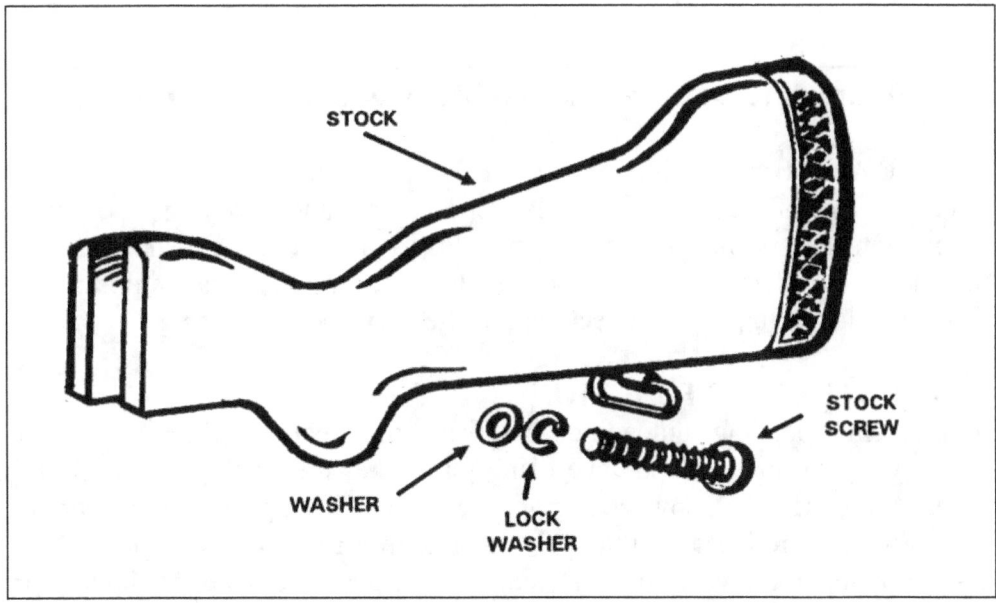

Figure A-11. Removing the stock.

A-7. CLEANING AND LUBRICATION
The grenadier cleans and lubricates the M79 grenade launcher the same as he would the M203 grenade launcher. (TM 9-1010-205-10 lists the tools and equipment required.)

A-8. GENERAL ASSEMBLY
The grenadier should assemble the grenade launcher in the reverse order in which he disassembled it (Figure A-12).

a. Place the lock washer on the stock screw and install the stock on the receiver.

b. Place the barrel on the fulcrum pin. Hold the cocking lever up, lower the barrel, and ensure that the cocking arm slides under the cocking lever. Close the barrel.

c. Place the fore-end assembly on the barrel and secure it by replacing the retaining band screw.

d. Replace the sling.

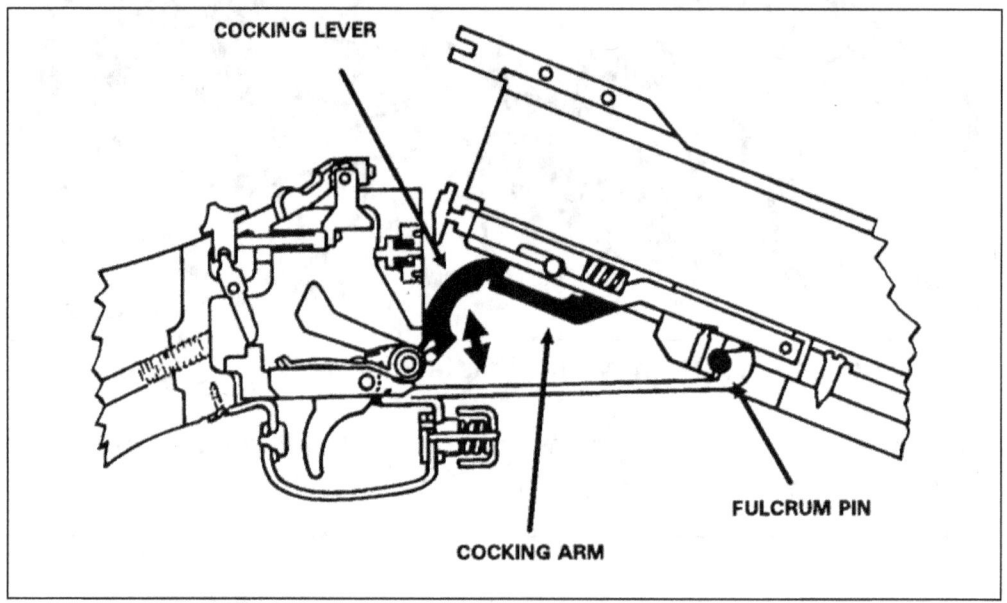

Figure A-12. Assembling the barrel and receiver groups.

A-9. CARE AND HANDLING

Proper maintenance of the M79 grenade launcher is vital and must be part of all gunnery training programs. Good maintenance contributes to weapon effectiveness as well as to unit readiness. Maintaining the weapon includes clearing, disassembling, cleaning, lubricating, and inspecting it, and checking its assembly and functions.

A-10. OPERATION AND FUNCTION

Operations include loading, unloading, and firing the weapon, which uses a high-low propulsion system to fire a round. The firing pin strikes the primer, whose flash ignites the propellant in the brass powder-charge cup inside the high-pressure chamber. The burning propellant produces 35,000 psi chamber pressure, which ruptures the brass powder-charge cup at the vent holes. This allows the gases to escape to the low-pressure chamber in the cartridge case, where the pressure drops to 3,000 psi and propels the grenade from the muzzle at a velocity of 250 fps. The grenade's 37,000-rpm right-hand spin stabilizes the grenade during flight and applies enough rotational force to arm the fuze. The grenadier loads and unloads the weapon with the barrel open and fires it from a closed bolt. The launcher must be cocked before it can be placed on SAFE.

a. **Loading**. To load the weapon (Figure A-13)--

(1) Move the barrel locking latch as far to the right as possible.

(2) Insert a round into the chamber, ensuring the extractor contacts the cartridge case rim.

(3) Close the weapon.
(4) Place the weapon on SAFE.

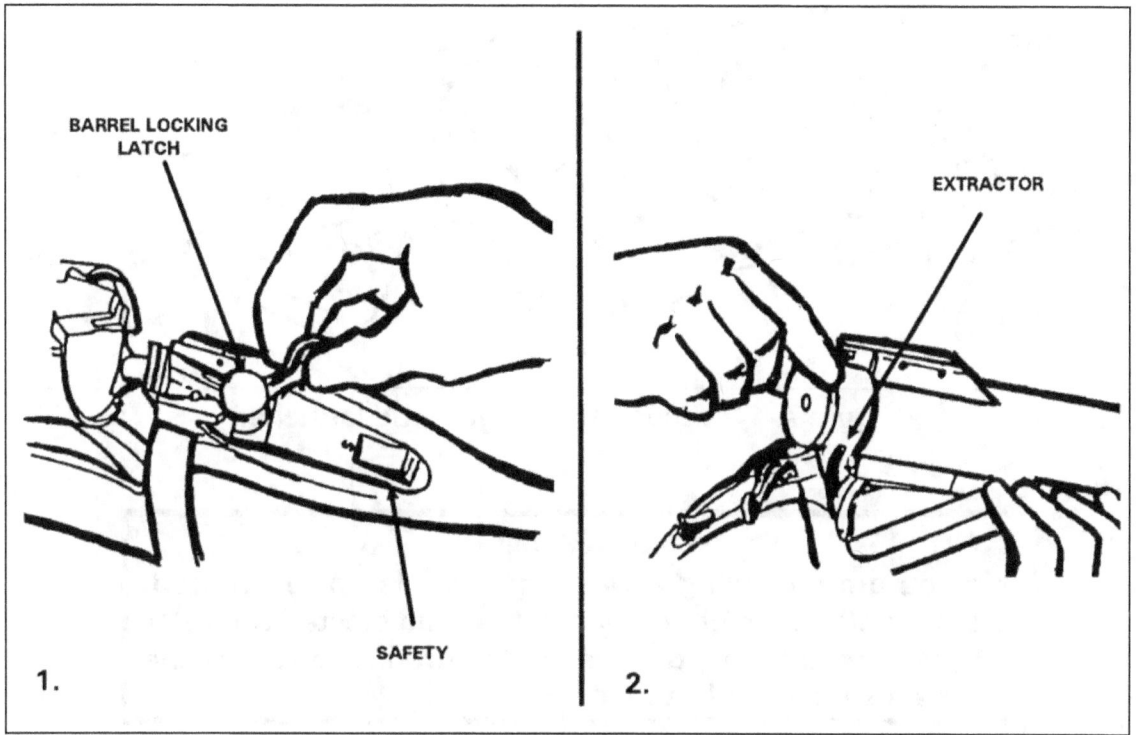

Figure A-13. Loading the grenade launcher.

WARNING

Keep the muzzle pointed downrange and clear of all soldiers. Use the correct ammunition; never use high-velocity 40-mm ammunition.

---

b. **Unloading**. To unload the weapon (Figure A-14)--

(1) Place the weapon on safe by moving the barrel locking latch as far right as possible.

(2) If the cartridge case is partially extracted, remove the cartridge case. If the cartridge case is not partially extracted, engage the extractor tang and pull it rearward.

(3) Grasp the cartridge case and remove it.

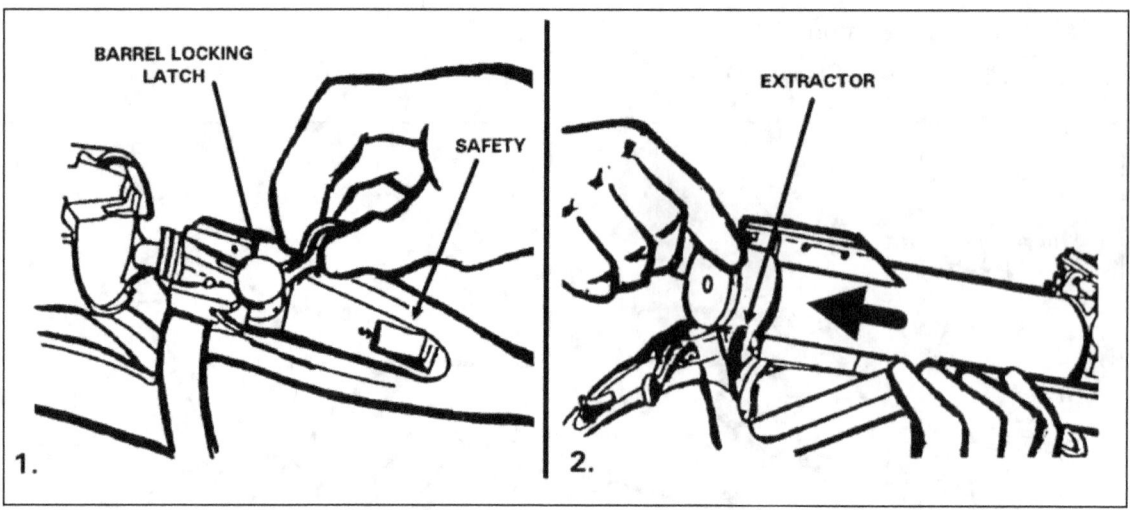

Figure A-14. Unloading the grenade launcher.

WARNING

If you are unloading a weapon that has not been fired, avoid detonation either by catching the ejected round or by holding the weapon close to the ground to reduce the distance the round can fall.

A-11. CYCLE OF FUNCTIONING

Understanding how the weapon functions helps grenadiers recognize and correct stoppages. The loading and firing of a round and the resulting effect on the parts of the weapon are referred to as the cycle of functioning. Many of the actions in this cycle occur at the same time and are separated here only to explain them more clearly.

a. **Unlocking**. Before you can unlock the barrel from the receiver and move the safety to the SAFE position, you must press the barrel locking latch lever all the way to the right. The spring-loaded latch lock holds the barrel locking latch open (Figure A-15, page A-12).

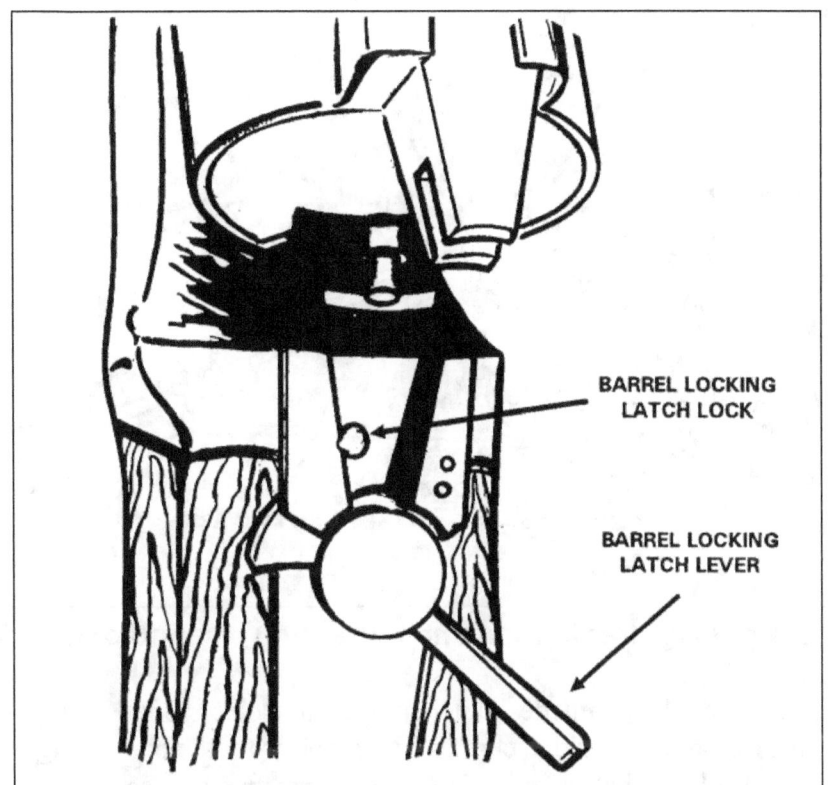

Figure A-15. Barrel release latch lock and barrel locking latch lever.

b. **Cocking**. Opening the barrel cocks the weapon by causing the cocking arm to lift the cocking lever. The cocking lever rotates around the hammer pin until it contacts a stud on the hammer. Then the lever rotates upward with the hammer until the sear engages the sear notch, cocking the weapon.

c. **Extracting**. Extraction occurs while you are cocking the weapon (Figure A-16). As you open the barrel, the spring-loaded extractor withdraws the spent cartridge case about 1/2 inch from the breech end of the barrel.

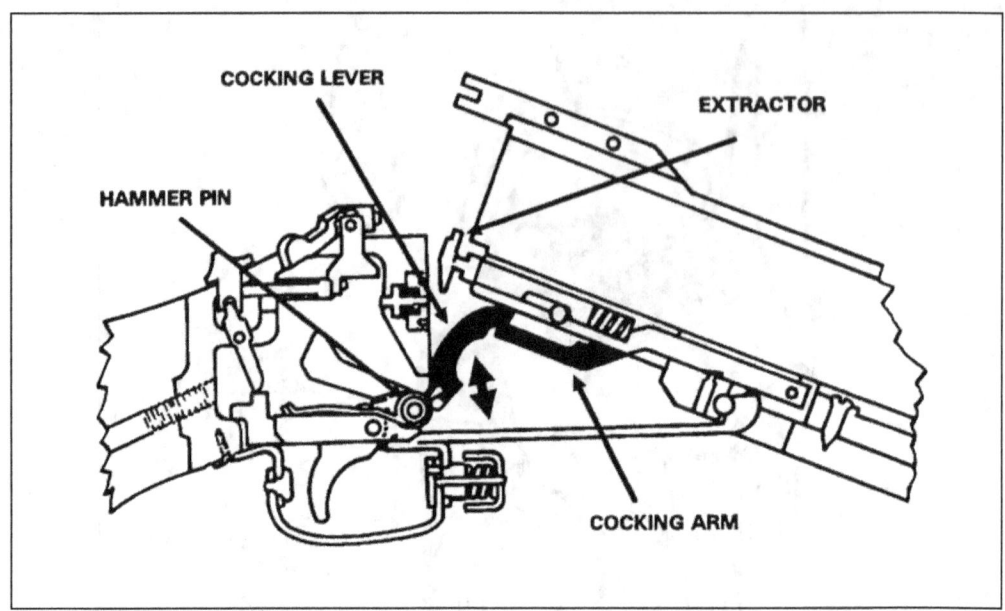

Figure A-16. Cocking the weapon and extracting a round or cartridge case.

d. **Ejecting**. The M79 grenade launcher does not eject rounds automatically; you must remove the expended cartridge case or live round from the barrel (Figure A-17).

e. **Loading**. With the barrel in the open position, insert a cartridge into the breech end of the barrel (Figure A-17).

Figure A-17. Loading the weapon or ejecting a round or cartridge case.

f. **Chambering**. Closing the barrel forces the extractor into the extractor housing, which causes the cartridge to seat in the chamber.

g. **Locking**. Closing the barrel also depresses the latch lock, which rotates until it locks the barrel to the receiver (when it engages the barrel locking lug). Before firing the weapon, you must push the safety forward to expose the letter "F."

h. **Firing**. As you pull the trigger rearward, it rotates on the trigger pin. The rear of the trigger lifts the rear of the sear, causing the nose of the sear to disengage from the sear notch in the hammer. This releases the spring-driven hammer, which strikes the firing pin and drives it forward to strike the primer of the cartridge. When you release the trigger, the hammer settles back slightly, allowing the firing pin spring to withdraw the pin from the face of the retainer (Figure A-18.).

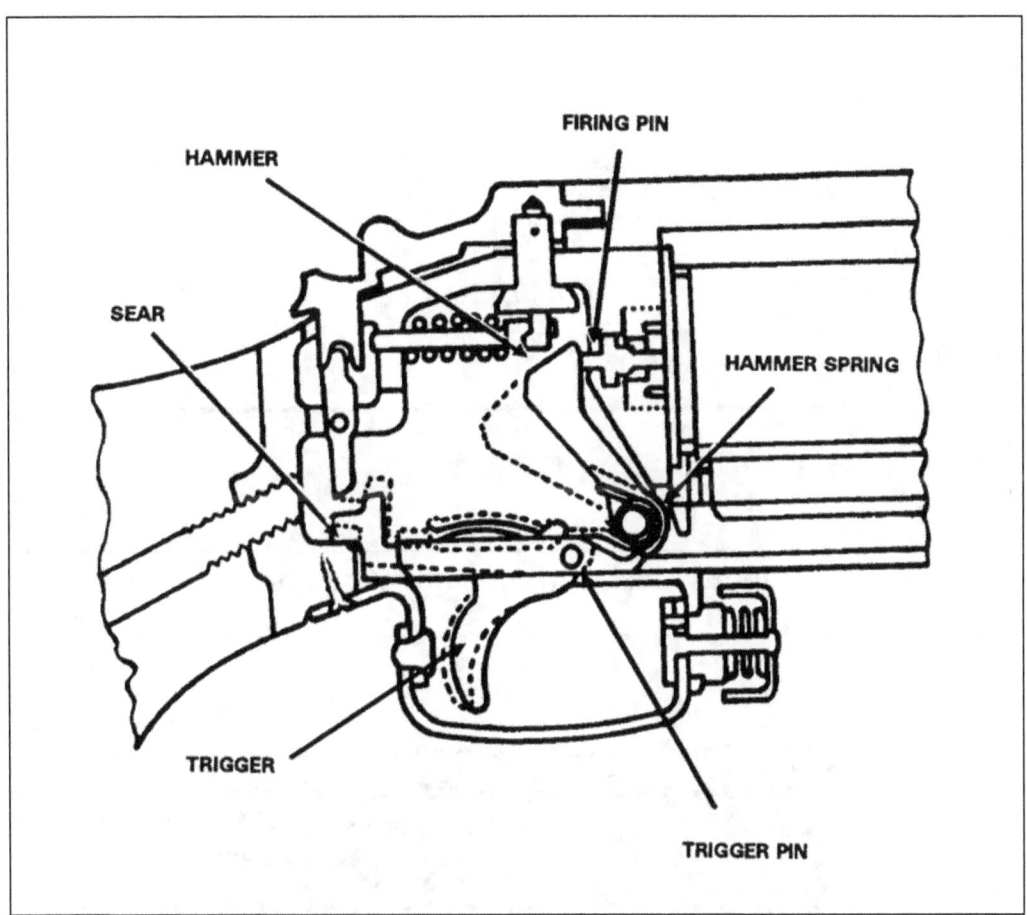

Figure A-18. Firing the weapon.

A-12. PERFORMANCE PROBLEMS AND DESTRUCTION

Performance problems and destruction procedures for the M79 grenade launcher are the same as for the M203 grenade launcher.

A-13. MARKSMANSHIP

Marksmanship training teaches the grenadier to fire the grenade launcher and prepares him to employ it in combat. Except for the subjects discussed in the remainder of this appendix, marksmanship training, range construction, and range firing are the same for the M79 grenade launcher as they are for the M203 grenade launcher.

a. **Sight Alignment, Sight Picture, and Sight Manipulation**. Sight alignment is the relationship between the front sight blade and the rear sight notch. Figure A-19 shows the correct sight alignment. If you drew an imaginary horizontal line across the top of the rear sight notch, the top of the front sight blade would touch the line. If you drew an imaginary vertical line through the center of the notch, the line would cut the front sight blade in half. Sight picture includes sight alignment and the placement of the aiming point (Figure A-20). Sight manipulation means placing the rear sight carrier at the elevation-scale setting that corresponds to the range to the target.

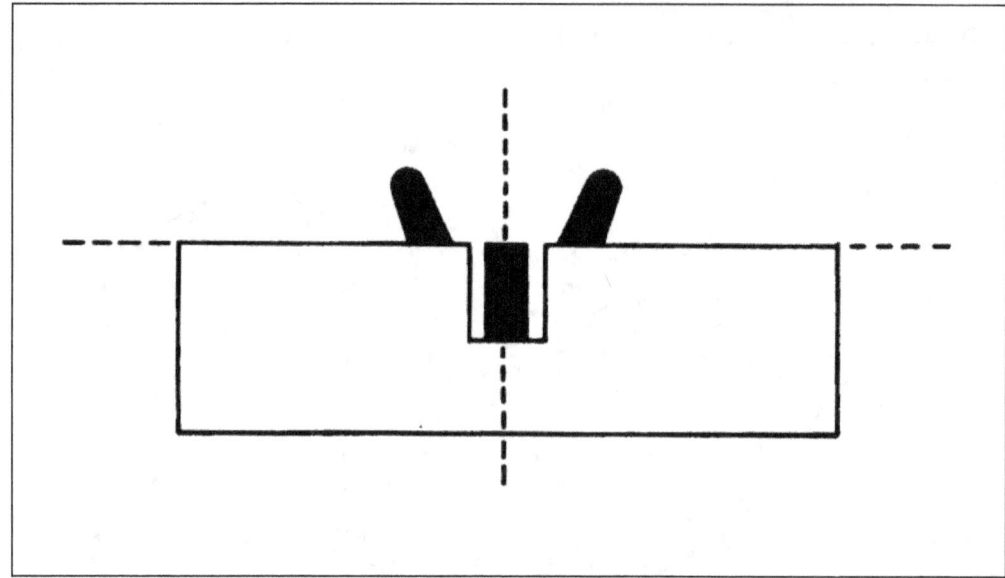

Figure A-19. Correct sight alignment.

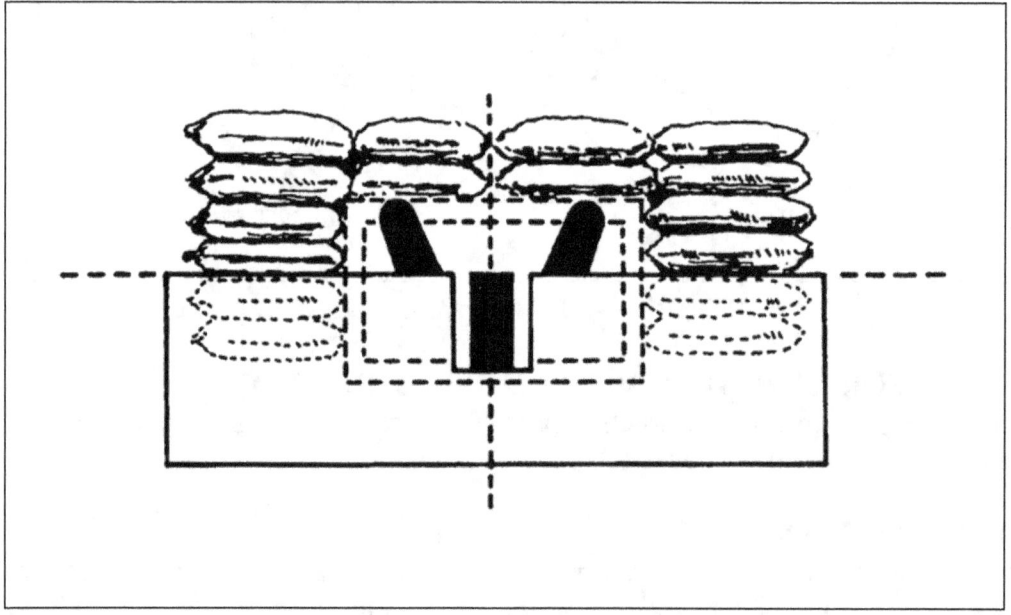

Figure A-20. Correct sight picture.

b. **Positions**. Firing positions for the M79 grenade launcher are the same as for the M203 grenade launcher. The ones you are most likely to use are the prone, kneeling, fighting, and standing positions. When you have an option, always use the more stable supported positions. Using the M79 in firing positions differs from using the M203 in the following ways:

(1) Assume firing positions the same as you would with your service rifle, but hold your right thumb against the right side of the grenade launcher's stock. If you place this thumb over the small of the stock, the safety can injure your thumb, and you will not achieve a spot weld with the grenade launcher.

(2) Several actions are common to all the firing positions for the M79 grenade launcher:

(a) Rest the launcher across the heel of your left hand, in the V formed by your left thumb and forefinger.

(b) Relax the fingers of your left hand, and place your hand so that the upper sling swivel cannot pinch it.

(c) Keep your left wrist straight, with your left thumb resting against the fore-end assembly--not on the rear sight base. Placing your thumb near the rear sight base could cause injury during firing.

(d) Place your left elbow under the launcher.

(e) Position your right elbow far enough to the right to level your shoulders and far enough forward to form a good pocket for the butt of the launcher.

(f) Rest the thumb of your right hand along the side of the stock.

WARNING
Do not place your thumb over the small of the stock. The safety could injure your thumb when the launcher recoils.

(g) Place your trigger finger on the trigger so that your finger and the side of the stock do not touch.

(h) Regardless of the firing position you have chosen, try to relax.

(3) At ranges less than 150 meters, you can fire normally from your shoulder in any position. However, to maintain sight alignment at greater ranges, lower the position of the stock on your shoulder or drop the butt from your shoulder. At near-maximum ranges, you must position the stock between your waist and your armpit and hold the stock firmly against your body with your upper arm. In the prone position, once the stock is no longer against your shoulder, rest the butt of the launcher on the ground. Be careful to keep your head level when your cheek breaks contact with the stock. Figure A-21 shows the changes that occur as the range to the target increases.

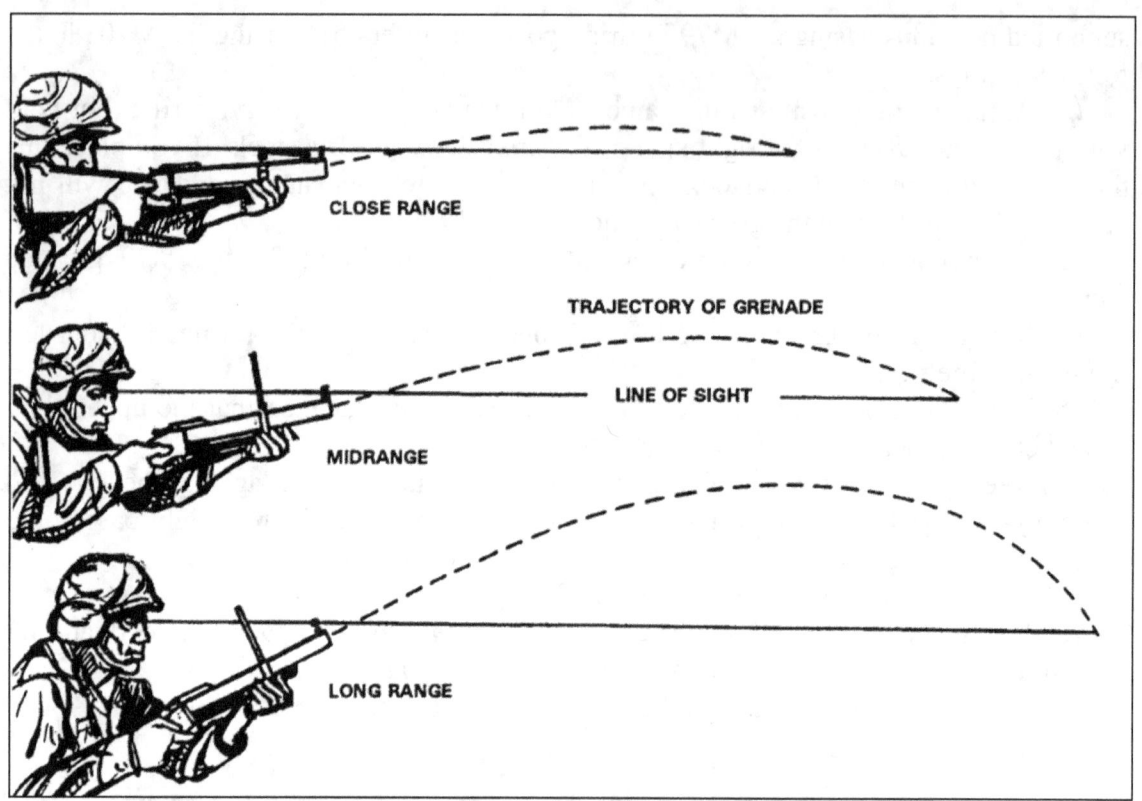

Figure A-21. Effect of increasing range.

(4) When pinpoint accuracy is not required, use the pointing technique to deliver a high rate of HE fire (Figure A-22, page A-18). The pointing technique uses a modified underarm firing position without using the sights. Keep both eyes open, concentrate on the target, and keep the muzzle of the launcher in position so you can easily adjust your fire. This technique is most useful in an assault because it allows you to reload rapidly with your left hand. However, you can use it in any standard firing position.

Figure A-22. Pointing technique.

c. **Zeroing Procedure**. You have achieved a correct zero for a given range when your elevation and windage settings enable you to hit the point of aim. To zero the M79 grenade launcher, engage a target at 200 meters. This range allows you the most flexibility to adjust elevation.

(1) Place the rear sight's center index line on the windage scale's center mark.

(2) Unlock the elevation scale by turning its lock screw counterclockwise. Position the top of the scale flush with the top of the sight frame and relock the scale. To unlock the rear sight carrier, turn and push the locknut that retains it. Slide the carrier along the elevation scale until the 200-meter index on the scale aligns with the top edge of the sight carrier. Relock the rear sight carrier.

(3) Assume a prone supported position and align the target with the front and rear sights, using correct sighting and aiming procedure.

(4) Fire a round, sense the impact of the grenade, and adjust the sight.

(a) *Elevation*. Turn the elevation screw wheel clockwise to increase the range, counterclockwise to decrease. At a range of 200 meters, one click on the wheel moves the impact of the grenade 2 1/2 meters.

(b) *Windage*. Turn the windage knob clockwise to move the impact of the grenade to the right, or counterclockwise to move left. At a range of 200 meters, one click on the knob moves the impact of the grenade about 11 inches.

(5) Fire two more rounds, and adjust after each. If the last round lands within 5 meters of the target, the weapon is correctly zeroed.

(6) After confirming the zero, move the elevation scale so that the 200-meter index line is flush with the top of the sight carrier.

A-14. INDIRECT FIRE ROLE

Although the M79 grenade launcher is designed for direct fire, it can be used to place HE fragmentation fire on area targets that cannot be observed.

a. **Employment**. The accuracy of the weapon is limited in the indirect fire role. Adjust the range, in 25-meter increments, to a maximum range of about 400 meters.

b. **Sighting System**. The standard sight assembly is graduated up to 375 meters, which corresponds to a 32-degree elevation. However, you can raise the rear sight carrier to increase elevation to up to 40 degrees. The rear sight cannot be used at greater elevations. The most accurate way to fire the M79 grenade launcher in the indirect fire mode is to attach an M15 rifle grenade sight to the weapon's stock (Figure A-23). This sight consists of a mounting scale plate and sight bar assembly.

Figure A-23. Using the M5 rifle grenade sight.

(1) *Installing the M15 Sight*. To prevent the wood in the launcher's stock from cracking when the sight is installed, hold the sight against the stock and mark the positions for the screws. Drill two pilot holes. Use two short wood screws and attach the mounting plate to the side of the stock. Ensure they do not protrude through the stock since this will make disassembling the weapon difficult.

(2) *Adjusting the M15 Sight*. Once you attach the M15 sight to the M79 grenade launcher, you will no longer need to use the mounting plate's degree scale. Place a short piece of masking tape on the stock above the mounting plate. Adjust your fires until the rounds impact at the desired range. After you determine the sight setting, draw a line on the tape along the top of the sight bar. Label each line for the appropriate range. Fire

several rounds to determine the M15 sight elevation graduation required to fire the desired range. Mark this graduation on the stock for quick reference.

(3) *Using the M15 Sight*. Align the launcher for deflection. Assume a correct firing position, sight over or along the barrel, and move the launcher to align the barrel toward the target. Ensure the weapon is not canted. Raise or lower the muzzle to center the leveling bubble and determine the angle of elevation. If you have enough light, using the M15 sight is the quickest, easiest way to determine the proper angle of elevation.

c. **Adjustments for Elevation and Deflection**. To bring indirect fire rounds nearer the target, move the barrel slightly for elevation or deflection.

(1) *Elevation*. Estimate the range to the target and move the barrel either up or down. Table A-1 provides guidelines to help you set the proper elevation.

Range	Elevation	Distance from Front Sling Swivel to Ground
200 meters	69 degrees	21 1/4 inches
300 meters	8 degrees	19 3/8 inches
400 meters	41 degrees	12 1/4 inches

Table A-1. Range estimation and elevation.

(2) *Deflection*. Sight over or along the barrel at an aiming point. To increase the accuracy of indirect fire, place a string or straight stick on the ground in line with an aiming point or stake.

d. **Ammunition**. Because live ammunition must be conserved during both training and combat, TP rounds are used for training and zeroing. A TP round emits a puff of orange or yellow smoke on impact, which will help you adjust fire. TP rounds produce little fragmentation, which reduces the possibility of a training injury.

e. **Wind and Other Weather Effects**. Firing any 40-mm grenade launcher round in the indirect fire role doubles the time required for the round to reach the target. This allows wind, snow, and rain twice the time to push the projectile off its normal trajectory. Before firing, you must evaluate and compensate for the wind, whether it is a crosswind or is blowing on the same axis as the grenade. This evaluation (referred to as "Kentucky windage") increases the chance of a first-round hit and reduces the chance that a round will impact closer to you than desired. Be careful when a wind of 5 mph or more is blowing from the direction of the target. Consider this particular wind condition when firing at all ranges, but remember that it presents the greatest danger at the minimum indirect fire range of 200 meters.

f. **Fire Control**. You may fire indirectly only when you receive a specific command to do so.

(1) Fire commands for indirect fire differ from those for direct fire only in that INDIRECT FIRE is given as the method of employment right after the target and range are designated.

    GRENADIER
    FRONT
    INDIRECT FIRE, 3 ROUNDS
    TROOPS IN OPEN

AT MY COMMAND

(2) If the indirect fire target is not visible from where you are, the squad leader may employ an observer.

(3) Grenade launcher fire-for-effect should always consist of three to five rounds, depending on the nature of the target.

g. **Firing Positions**. You may fire the M79 grenade launcher indirectly from the kneeling, sitting, or squatting position.

(1) *Kneeling*. The kneeling position for indirect fire is about the same as for direct fire (Figure A-24).

(a) Face the target and kneel on your right knee (if you are firing right-handed), keeping your left foot pointed in the direction of the target.

(b) Sit on your right heel and place the butt of the stock on the ground against or alongside your right knee.

(c) With your left hand, grasp the launcher near the upper sling swivel. With your right, grasp the small of the stock. Your right thumb should be parallel to your trigger finger and against the right side of the stock. The weight of your body should rest on your right heel.

Figure A-24. Kneeling position using the marked-sling method.

(2) *Sitting*. The sitting position for indirect fire is about the same as for direct fire. Use this position with aiming stakes or with the M15 sight (Figure A-25).

(a) Keep your right leg flat on the ground and pointed at the target, crossing your left leg over your knee so your left knee supports your left elbow.

(b) Place the butt of the stock alongside your right hip.

(c) Hold the weapon as described for the indirect fire kneeling position.

Figure A-25. Sitting position for indirect fire.

(3) *Squatting*. If you must remain in an indirect fire position for any length of time, squatting is the least comfortable. It is identical to the direct fire modified squatting position except for one difference: place the weapon between your knees, with the butt of the stock on the ground (Figure A-26). Hold the launcher as described for the kneeling position. Use aiming stakes or the M15 sight with this position.

Figure A-26. Squatting position for indirect fire.

h. **Methods of Fire**. Three methods may be used to fire the M79 indirectly.

(1) *Marked-Sling Method*. This is the most field-expedient method. Loosen the sling, assume a kneeling position, and place your forward foot in the sling (Figure A-24, page A-21). Before firing, ensure that the sling is taut and vertical between the front sling swivel and your boot. If not, the rounds will impact at a greater range than you desire. To ensure the sling is vertical, tie one end of a piece of string to the front sling swivel and the other end to a weight such as a cartridge case. Align the edge of the sling with the string. Fire several rounds to determine the desired range. Use tape, paint, ink, or a similar material to mark the sling where your foot is holding it to the ground. Mark the position of the sling keeper and buckle so that if either is moved, you can return it to its original position to ensure constant range accuracy. Remember that the sling may stretch or shrink if it gets wet, which will increase or decrease the range to impact.

(2) *Aiming Stakes Method*. If you use aiming stakes, you can deliver planned indirect fire (Figure A-27, page A-24). Place the aiming stakes and verify their alignment in daylight. Record planned fires on a range card or sector sketch. Then place the fore-end assembly of the weapon on top of an elevation support, scooping a slight depression out of the ground for the toe of the weapon's stock. Adjust the weapon for the range desired; then drive a stake into the ground behind the toe of the stock to absorb recoil and prevent the weapon from digging into the ground. To control the barrel's lateral movement, place two deflection stakes behind the front elevation support. Place another elevation support beneath the stock of the weapon and two more deflection stakes behind the support to control the stock's lateral movement. Place the deflection stakes closer together than the front stakes.

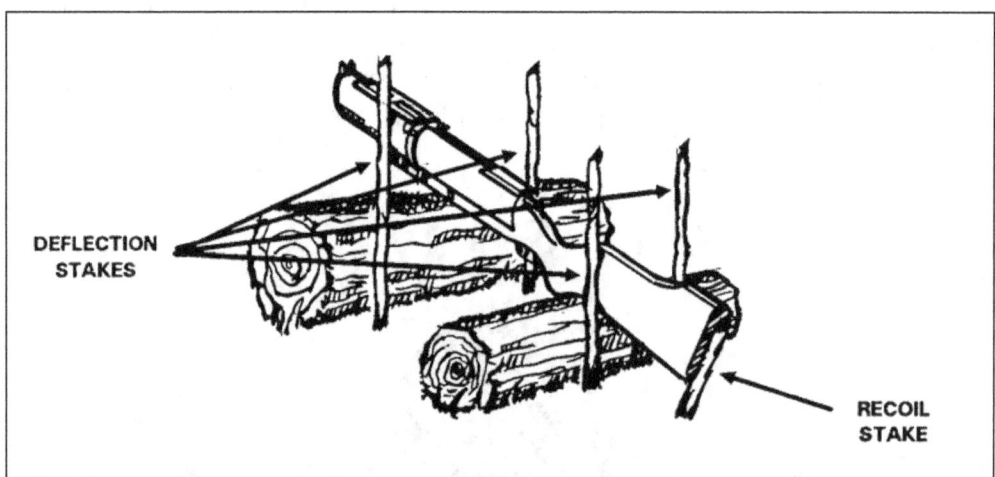

DEFLECTION
STAKES

RECOIL
STAKE

Figure A-27. Planned fires using aiming stakes.

i. **Safety Precautions**. The grenadier should observe the following safety precautions in addition to those stated in AR 385-63 and in local range regulations:

(1) Keep your head behind and below the muzzle of the launcher when firing.

(2) Ensure sufficient overhead clearance exists for indirect fire. Remember that some rounds arm themselves 14 to 28 meters from the muzzle of the launcher.

(3) Fire no rounds at less than 200 meters.

APPENDIX B
UNIT TRAINING PROGRAM

This appendix provides guidance for conducting unit marksmanship training and the marksmanship proficiency examination.

B-1. SEQUENCE OF TRAINING
The segments of the unit training program are conducted in the following order:
a. Introduction.
b. Preliminary marksmanship instruction and dry fire.
c. Practice qualification.
d. Day record firing (includes NBC record firing).
e. Night record firing.

B-2. INTRODUCTION
Trainers briefly describe the weapon and its history. Then they conduct the actual training. The total time allotted for this segment of the unit training program is 3 hours and 15 minutes.
a. **Disassembly and Assembly**. Specific time allotments are as follows:
(1) Detailed disassembly requires 25 minutes.
(2) Operator maintenance, to include inspecting, cleaning, and lubricating (10 minutes each), requires a total of 30 minutes.
(3) Detailed assembly requires 25 minutes.
(4) Detailed disassembly and assembly require 50 minutes. (An optional practice exercise requires additional time.)
b. **General Data**. Specific time allotments are as follows:
(1) Minimum and maximum ranges require 15 minutes.
(2) Identification of the five standard types of 40-mm ammunition and their purposes requires 30 minutes.
(3) Target engagement requires 10 minutes each for area and point targets (20 minutes total).

B-3. PRELIMINARY MARKSMANSHIP INSTRUCTION AND DRY FIRE
Trainers briefly describe this segment of the unit training program. The total time allotted for this segment is 3 hours.
a. **Fundamentals of Marksmanship**. This has three parts:
(1) Assuming proper position and grip, aiming, and squeezing the trigger requires 30 minutes.
(2) Loading, reducing stoppages, and clearing the weapon requires 30 minutes.
(3) Zeroing requires 30 minutes.
b. **Dry-Fire Practice**. This also has three parts:
(1) Aiming requires 30 minutes.
(2) Setting and changing the sight requires 30 minutes.
(3) Zeroing requires 30 minutes.

B-4. PROFICIENCY (PERFORMANCE) EXAMINATION

Trainers use the proficiency examination to test and evaluate what soldiers have already learned. The time allotted for this segment is 1 hour.

B-5. DAY RECORD FIRING

The total time needed for each firing order is 1 hour and 18 minutes. The ammunition requirement for Firing Table I is 20 rounds of TP.

a. Reviewing preliminary marksmanship, which includes aim, sight picture, and trigger control, requires 30 minutes.

b. Conducting the function check, loading, applying immediate action, clearing, and observing range safety require 15 minutes.

c. Introducing grenade launcher firing, which includes sensing, adjusting sights, acquiring targets, and scoring targets, requires 15 minutes total.

d. Conducting day record fire (Firing Table I) requires 18 minutes.

B-6. 25-METER FIRING AND NIGHT RECORD FIRING

The time allotted for this segment of the unit training program is 2 hours and 15 minutes.

a. Introducing this segment, which covers 25-meter firing with the AN/PVS-4, requires 15 minutes.

b. Grouping and zeroing require 1 hour.

c. Conducting night record fire (Firing Table II) requires 1 hour. The ammunition requirement for this firing table is 3 rounds of HE.

APPENDIX C
PROFICIENCY (PERFORMANCE) EXAMINATION

This appendix provides the examination used to test soldiers' proficiency with the M203 grenade launcher in dry-fire tasks.

C-1. DESCRIPTION

The examination is a practical nonfiring exercise given during the last period of M203 training before range firing. Trainers need not conduct this examination on a range and may conduct it indoors if facilities are available. Soldiers must demonstrate proper techniques for the following tasks:

    a. Perform general disassembly and assembly.

    b. Set the sights.

    c. Identify five standard types of 40-mm ammunition and their purposes.

    d. Load, unload, and place the M203 grenade launcher on SAFE.

    e. Apply immediate action.

C-2. CONDUCT OF EXAMINATION

This paragraph explains how to conduct the examination. The suggested times may help the commander plan the examination.

    a. **Equipment**. The following equipment is required to conduct the proficiency examination:

    (1) *Tables*. At station 3, set up one table for every three soldiers being tested. At each of the other stations, set up only one table. Ensure every table has an ample supply of paper and pencils.

    (2) *Setups*. At each station, prepare one "setup" for each soldier to be tested. A setup consists of everything one soldier needs to complete the task for that station.

    (3) *Weapons*. Except at station 3, include one M203 grenade launcher in each setup.

    (4) *Dummy Ammunition*. Provide twelve rounds of dummy ammunition for each setup at stations 1 and 2 and one round of dummy ammunition for each setup at stations 4 and 5. Station 3 does not require dummy ammunition.

    b. **Time Allocation**. Time required for the examination should not exceed 3 1/2 hours if allocated as follows:

- 15 minutes total for the orientation, instructions, breakdown, and movement.
- 30 minutes at each of the five stations (total of 2 1/2 hours).
- Two 10-minute breaks (20 minutes).
- Five 5-minute movement periods (25 minutes).

C-3. STATIONS

Five subjects and stations are recommended for this proficiency examination. This paragraph describes each station and its requirements. Figures containing the score sheets follow at the end of this appendix.

a. **Station 1--Perform General Disassembly and Assembly**.

(1) Prepare one setup for each soldier to be tested. Each setup should include one M203 grenade launcher with its breech closed and its safety on SAFE. Place each weapon on a mat to keep its parts free of dirt.

(2) Trainers should read the following statement:

> *During this period, you will be organized into three groups and required to disassemble and assemble the M203 grenade launcher. There will be one grader for every two weapons. You will have 8 minutes to complete the general disassembly and assembly. If you have any trouble, raise your hand and the grader will assist you. When your group is not being tested, remain to the rear of the station with your back toward the working area until your group is called.*

(3) Trainers use the checklist shown in Figure C-1 on page C-4 to grade individual performance.

(4) After each group is tested, trainers assemble the soldiers they graded and critique them thoroughly (for about 5 minutes).

b. **Station 2--Set the Sights**.

(1) Prepare one setup for each soldier to be tested. Each setup should include one M203 grenade launcher with its breech open and its safety on SAFE. Place each weapon on a mat to keep its parts free of dirt.

(2) Trainers read the following statement:

> *During this period, you will be organized into three groups and required to set the quadrant and sight leaf for range and windage. There will be one grader for every two weapons. You will have 4 minutes to set each sight. If you have any trouble, raise your hand and the grader will assist you. When your group is not being tested, remain to the rear of the station with your back toward the working area until your group is called.*

(3) Trainers use the checklist shown in Figure C-2 on page C-4 to grade individual performance.

(4) After each group is tested, trainers assemble the soldiers they graded and critique them thoroughly (for about 5 minutes).

c. **Station 3--Identify Five Standard Types of 40-mm Ammunition and their Purposes**.

(1) Prepare one table for every three soldiers. Each soldier's setup should consist of ample paper and pencils.

(2) Trainers read the following statement:

During this period, you will be organized into three groups and required to identify five standard types of 40-mm ammunition and their purposes. There will be one grader for every two tables. You will have 10 minutes to complete the task. If you have any trouble, raise your hand and the grader will assist you. When you are not being tested, remain to the rear of the station with your back toward the working area until you are called.

(3) Trainers use the checklist shown in Figure C-3 on page C-5 to grade individual performance.

(4) After testing each group, trainers assemble the soldiers they graded and critique them thoroughly (for about 5 minutes).

    d. **Station 4--Load, Unload, and Place the M203 Grenade Launcher on SAFE.**

(1) Prepare one setup for each soldier to be tested. Each setup should include one dummy round and one M203 grenade launcher with its breech closed and its safety on FIRE. Place each weapon on a mat to keep its parts free of dirt.

(2) Trainers read the following statement:

During this period, you will be organized into three groups and required to load, unload, and place the M203 grenade launcher on SAFE. There will be one grader. You will have 2 minutes to complete the task. If you have any trouble, raise your hand and the grader will assist you. When your group is not being tested, remain to the rear of the station with your back toward the working area until your group is called.

(3) Trainers use the checklist shown in Figure C-4 on page C-5 to grade individual performance.

(4) After testing each group, trainers assemble the soldiers they graded and critique them thoroughly (for about 5 minutes).

    e. **Station 5--Apply Immediate Action**.

(1) Prepare one setup for each soldier to be tested. Each setup should include one dummy round and one M203 grenade launcher with its breech open and its safety on SAFE. Place each weapon on a mat to keep its parts free of dirt.

(2) Trainers read the following statement:

During this period, you will be organized into three groups and required to apply immediate action. There will be one grader. You will have 2 minutes to complete the task. If you have any trouble, raise your hand, and the grader will assist you. When your group is not being tested, remain to the rear of the station with your back toward the working area until your group is called.

(3) Trainers use the checklist shown in Figure C-5 on page C-5 to grade individual performance.

(4) After testing each group, trainers assemble the soldiers they graded and critique them thoroughly (for about 5 minutes).

STATION 1

<u>CHECKLIST</u>
Clear the M203 grenade launcher:
☐ 1. Cock the weapon, observe for extraction, place the safety in the safe position, inspect the breech, and return the barrel to the FIRE position.

Disassemble the M203 grenade launcher:
☐ 2. Remove the quadrant sight.
☐ 3. Pull back the slip ring. Lift up on the handguard and pull it to the rear to remove it.
☐ 4. Press the barrel latch and move the barrel forward to the barrel stop.
☐ 5. Unlock the opening of the M203 grenade launcher barrel.
☐ 6. Press the barrel stop to release the barrel from the receiver and remove the barrel.

Assemble the M203 grenade launcher:
☐ 7. Replace the barrel, press the barrel stop, and slide the barrel into the receiver.
☐ 8. Move the barrel rearward to close it.
☐ 9. Replace the handguard and secure it with the slip ring.
☐ 10. Replace the quadrant sight.

Perform a function check on the M203 grenade launcher:
☐ 11. Cock the launcher and pull the trigger. Hold the trigger to the rear and cock the launcher again. Release the trigger and then pull it. Check the safety in both SAFE and FIRE positions. Check the leaf sight windage adjustment screw and the function of the barrel latch.

Figure C-1. Station 1--Perform general disassembly and assembly.

STATION 2

<u>CHECKLIST</u>
Set first sight:
☐ 1. Place the sight in an upright position.
☐ 2. Index the windage scale.
☐ 3. Index the elevation adjustment screw.
☐ 4. Tighten the elevation adjustment screw.
☐ 5. Assume a prone supported position.
☐ 6. Set the sight for the range given and align the sight with the target.

Set second sight:
☐ 1. Ensure the sight is correctly mounted.
☐ 2. Open the front sight post and rear sight aperture.
☐ 3. Align the rear sight aperture with the index line.
☐ 4. Move the front sight post to its highest position; then move it back 2 1/2 turns.
☐ 5. Assume a supported prone position.
☐ 6. Set the sight for the range given and align the sight with the target.

Figure C-2. Station 2--Set the sights.

STATION 3

CHECKLIST
- ☐ 1. Identify an M433 high-explosive dual-purpose round and state its purpose.
- ☐ 2. Identify an M406 high-explosive round and state its purpose.
- ☐ 3. Identify an M781 training practice round and state its purpose.
- ☐ 4. Identify an M583A1 star parachute round and state its purpose.
- ☐ 5. Identify an M713 ground marker round and state its purpose.

**Figure C-3. Station 3--Identify five standard types of
40-mm ammunition and their purposes.**

STATION 4

CHECKLIST
Load the M203 grenade launcher:
- ☐ 1. Open the breech and place the weapon on safe.
- ☐ 2. Insert a 40-mm round into the chamber.
- ☐ 3. Close the breech and ensure it locks.

Unload the M203 grenade launcher:
- ☐ 4. Depress the barrel latch and open the breech.
- ☐ 5. Hold one hand under the barrel to catch the extracted round.
- ☐ 6. Place the weapon on safe.
- ☐ 7. Slide the barrel to the rear to close the breech.

**Figure C-4. Station 4--Load, unload, and place the
M203 grenade launcher on SAFE.**

STATION 5

CHECKLIST
- ☐ 1. Load the M203 grenade launcher and try to fire.
- ☐ 2. Announce a misfire and keep the weapon pointed at the target.
- ☐ 3. Wait 30 seconds and clear the area before trying to unload the weapon.
- ☐ 4. Use extreme caution during unloading.
- ☐ 5. Determine whether the primer is dented (round is at fault) or not (firing mechanism is at fault).

Figure C-5. Station 5--Apply immediate action.

APPENDIX D
RANGE SAFETY

This appendix recommends safety precautions for the range described in this manual. This information, however, does not replace AR 385-63 or local regulations. In addition, safety requirements vary due to the differences between range courses of fire.

D-1. MARKSMANSHIP TRAINING
The following safety precautions must be observed during all marksmanship training:

a. **Trainers**.

(1) Display a red flag at the entrance to the range or in some other prominent location on the range to warn soldiers that live-fire range training is in progress.

(2) Mark firing limits with red and white striped poles that are visible to all firers.

(3) Ensure communications equipment such as microphones, PA systems, loudspeakers, and radios are in good working condition.

(4) Keep all weapons that are not in use safeguarded properly in a prescribed area.

(5) Prohibit smoking near ammunition, explosives, or flammables.

b. **Trainers and Soldiers**.

(1) Always assume that weapons are loaded until they have been examined and found to contain no ammunition.

(2) Never place obstructions in the muzzles of weapons about to be fired.

(3) Wear hearing protection during firing.

D-2. RANGE TRAINING
The range is dangerous. Whether conducting range training or participating in it, everyone must remain alert and observe safety precautions. Trainers and soldiers have specific safety responsibilities.

a. **Before Firing**. Trainers and soldiers have the following safety responsibilities before firing.

(1) *Trainers*. Trainers have the following safety responsibilities before range firing:

(a) Close all prescribed roadblocks and barriers and post necessary guards.

(b) Brief all personnel on the firing limits of range and firing lanes.

(c) Obtain range clearance from the installation range-control office.

(d) Check downrange before firing to ensure all personnel and equipment are clear.

(e) Keep a complete first-aid kit on the range.

(f) Locate medical personnel nearby where they can be contacted quickly.

(g) Check all weapons to ensure they are operational.

(h) Draw ammunition and issue it only on command of the OIC. When two or more lots of ammunition are used for firing, the OIC ensures the lots are separated and properly identified in case of accident or malfunction.

(i) Do not allow anyone to move forward of the firing line without permission of the tower operator, safety officer, or OIC.

(2) *Trainers and Soldiers*. Trainers and soldiers share the following safety responsibilities before range firing:

(a) Check all weapons to ensure they are clear of ammunition and obstructions and that their covers are up to show they are clear.

(b) Do not handle weapons except on command from the tower operator or OIC.

(c) Protect all ammunition from the direct rays of the sun.

b. **During Basic Firing**. Trainers and soldiers have the following safety responsibilities during basic firing:

(1) *Trainers*. Trainers are solely responsible for ensuring no one goes forward of the firing line due to the danger posed by duds.

(2) *Trainers and Soldiers*. Trainers and soldiers share the following responsibilities during basic firing:

(a) If anyone observes an unsafe condition, they should immediately call CEASE FIRE. Do not resume firing until directed by the OIC.

(b) When rounds fail to ignite or explode, they are referred to as duds. When this occurs, record the range (in meters) and the type of ammunition used. Submit this information to range control personnel.

c. **When Clearing the Weapon**. Trainers and soldiers have the following safety responsibilities when clearing the weapon:

(1) *Soldier*.

(a) Cock the weapon, observe the extraction of the round, and place the safety on SAFE.

(b) Inspect the breech to ensure that no round is present. If clear, announce CHAMBER CLEAR.

(2) *Assistant Instructor*.

(a) Run a cleaning rod through the barrel until you see the end of the rod in the receiver.

(b) Withdraw the rod.

(3) *Soldier*.

(a) If the gun is clear, return the barrel assembly to the firing position.

(b) Take the safety off SAFE and pull the trigger.

(c) Cock the weapon.

(d) Return the barrel assembly to the firing position.

(e) Place the safety on SAFE.

d. **During Limited Visibility**. Trainers have the following responsibilities during range firing in limited visibility:

(1) Check the down-range area before firing to ensure that all personnel and equipment are clear of the area. To do this, ask three times over a PA system, "Is there anyone downrange?" Each time, pause long enough to permit a response.

(2) Mark the range at its entrance or another prominent location with a blinking red light in addition to the red flag.

(3) Mount two red lights on the striped poles that mark the limits of fire. These lights must be visible to all firers.

(4) Do not allow anyone to move from his position until directed by the OIC.

e. **After Firing**. Trainers have the following responsibilities after range firing:

(1) Have safety personnel inspect all weapons to ensure that they are clear.

(2) Determine if soldiers have any expended cartridges or live ammunition.

(3) Keep weapons that are clear in a prescribed area with their barrel assemblies open and their safeties on SAFE.

APPENDIX E
STANDARDS, STRATEGIES, AND REQUIREMENTS

This appendix provides weapons training standards, training strategies, and resource requirements for the M203 grenade launcher. Category I (Figure E-1) applies to soldiers with an 11B or 11M military occupational specialty assigned to an infantry rifle platoon or 19D or 11B assigned to a scout platoon or long-range surveillance detachment. Category II (Figure E-2 on page E-2) applies to all other solider not identified as Category I. Refer to DA Pam 350-38, Chapter 5, for further explanation.

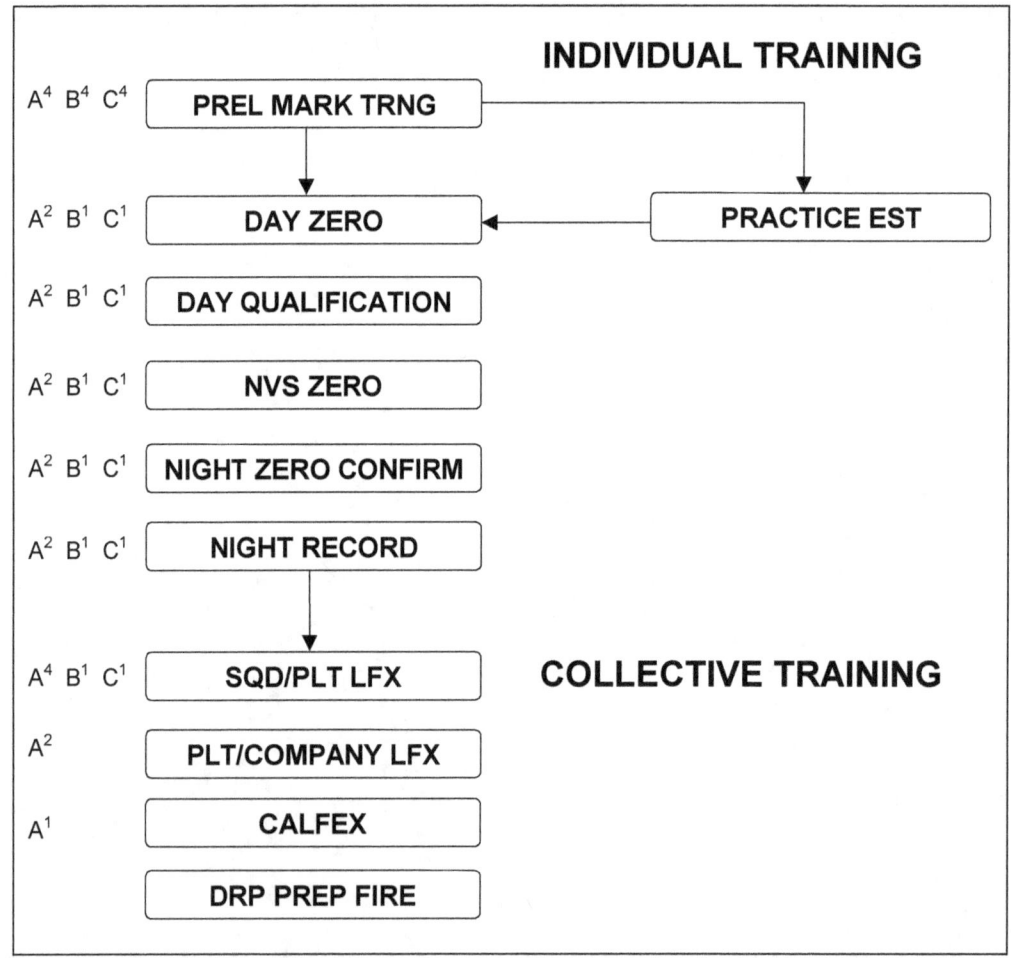

Figure E-1. M203 ammunition/training strategy (Category I).

EVENT	ROUNDS PER EVENT	FREQUENCY BY TRC				DODIC
		A	B	C	D	
Preliminary Marksmanship Training	EST	4	4	2	4	
Night Zero	12 BALL	1	0.5^1	0	0	
Night Confirmation[5]	3 TP	1	0.5^1	0	0	
Night Record Fire	3 HE	1	0.5^1	0	0	
Zero[3] Confirmation both sights[2]	10	1	1	1	1	
Qualification[3]	15 TP	1	1	0	0.5^1	
LFX	4 TP	1	0	0	0	
DRF Prep Fire[4]	6 TP					
		Total Rounds Per Weapon				
	HE	3	$3/0^6$	0	0	B546
	TP	12	$24/21^6$	6	$21/6^6$	B519
	BALL	12	$12/0^6$	0	0	A071/ A059

Notes:

1. Biennial events.

2. Zero quadrant sight using 3 TP rounds; zero leaf sight using 3 TP rounds; then qualify IAW FM 3-22.31.

3. TP will not be substituted for HE during night qualification.

4. DRF Prep Fire--6 TP--Request based on frequency of alert status.

5. Zero night vision devices to weapon.

6. Biennial event fired/Biennial event not fired.

Figure E-2. M203 ammunition/training strategy (Category II).

GLOSSARY

AAR	after-action review
ammo	ammunition
C	Centigrade
CLP	cleaner, lubricant, preservative
cm	centimeter(s)
CMF	career management field
CS	a chemical agent (tear gas)
DA	Department of the Army
DODAC	Department of Defense Ammunition Code
EST	engagement skills trainer
F	Fahrenheit
FM	field manual
FOV	field of view
FPL	final protective line
fps	feet per second
FTX	field training exercise
HE	high explosive
HEDP	high-explosive dual-purpose
hr	hour(s)
IAW	in accordance with
IET	initial entry training
IOAC	Infantry officer advanced course
IOBC	Infantry officer basic course
IET	initial entry training
KD	known-distance (range)
kg	kilogram(s)
kps	kilometers per second
LFX	live-fire exercise
LTA	local training area
METL	mission-essential task list
m	meter(s)
min	minute(s)
mm	millimeter(s)
MOPP	mission-oriented protective posture
MOUT	military operations on urbanized terrain

mph	mile(s) per hour
mps	meter(s) per second
MTA	major training area
MTP	mission training plan
NBC	nuclear, biological, chemical
NCO	noncommissioned officer
NCOES	Noncommissioned Officer Education System
NCOIC	noncommissioned officer in charge
NSN	national stock number
NVD	night vision device
OAC	officer advanced course
OBC	officer basic course
OIC	officer in charge (of)
OGIVE	head of the round
PD	point-detonating
PDF	principal direction of fire
PMT	preparatory marksmanship training
psi	pounds per square inch
RETS	remoted target system
rpm	revolution(s) per minute
S2	Intelligence Officer
S3	Operations and Training Officer
S4	Supply Officer
SEE	small emplacement excavator
SM	soldier's manual
SMCT	soldier's manual of common tasks
SOP	standing operating procedure
SSN	social security number
STP	soldier training publication
STX	situational training exercise
TP	training practice
TRADOC	Army Training and Doctrine Command
TRC	training readiness condition

INDEX

REFERENCES

SOURCES USED

These are the sources quoted or paraphrased in this publication. All are US Army publications unless stated otherwise.

FM 3-3 — Chemical and Biological Contamination Avoidance. 16 November 1992.

FM 3-4 — NBC Protection. 29 May 1992.

FM 21-60 — Visual Signals. 30 September 1987.

FM 3-5 — NBC Decontamination. 28 July 2000.

FM 21-75 — Combat Skills of the Soldier. 3 August 1984.

FM 23-9 — M16A1 Rifle and M16A2 Rifle Marksmanship. 3 July 1989.

STP 7-11BCHM14-SM-TG — Soldier's Manual, Skill Levels 1234, and Trainer's Guide, CMF 11, Infantry. 30 September 1988.

STP 21-1-SMCT — Soldier's Manual of Common Tasks, Skill Level 1. 1 October 1990.

TC 25-8 — Training Ranges, 25 February 1992, with Change 1, 16 November 1992.

TM 9-1010-221-10 — Operator's Manual for 40-mm Grenade Launcher, M203. 17 December 1984.

TM 9-1010-221-23&P — Unit and Direct Support Maintenance Manual, Including Repair Parts and Special Tools List, for Launcher, Grenade, 40-mm, M203. 12 January 1993.

TM 43-0001-28 — Army Ammunition Data Sheets for Artillery Ammunition: Guns, Howitzers, Mortars, Recoilless Rifles, Grenade Launchers, and Artillery Fuzes. 25 April 1977.

TM 750-244-7 — Procedures for Destruction of Equipment In Federal Supply Classifications 1000, 1005, 1010, 1015, 1020, 1025, 1030, 1055, 1090, and 1095 To Prevent Enemy Use. 18 June 1970.

DOCUMENTS NEEDED

These documents must be available to the intended users of this publication.

AR 385-63	Policies and Procedures for Firing Ammunition for Training, Target Practice, and Combat. 15 October 1983.
DA Form 2946-R	40-mm Grenade Launcher Scorecard. August 1994.
TRADOC Pam	Standards in Weapons Training. 03 July 1997.
TRADOC Reg 350-6	Initial Entry Training (IET) Policies and Administration. 30 November 1998.

INTERNET WEB SITES

U.S. Army Publishing Agency
http://www.usapa.army.mil

Army Doctrine and Training Digital Library
http://www.adtdl.army.mil/root/cgisearch.htm

40-MM GRENADE LAUNCHER SCORECARD

For use of this form, see FM 3-23.31, chapter 5; the proponent agency is TRADOC.

DATA REQUIRED BY THE PRIVACY ACT OF 1974

AUTHORITY: 10 USC 3012(g)/Executive Order 9397.

PRINCIPAL PURPOSE(S): Record individual performance.

ROUTINE USES: Evaluate individual proficiency and determine proficiency level. SSN is used for positive identification purposes only.

DISCLOSURE: Voluntary. Individuals not providing information cannot be rated or scored on a mass basis.

NAME: _____   QUALIFICATION RATING: _____

SSN: _____   DATE: _____   GRADE: _____

ORGANIZATION: _____

| | ZERO LEAF SIGHT: | DEFILADE | ELEVATION | | ZERO QUADRANT SIGHT: | DEFILADE | ELEVATION |

TASK NUMBER	DAY AND NBC RECORD FIRE	TIME
1	TGT 1 HIT _____ MISS _____ POINTS _____ TGT 2 HIT _____ MISS _____ POINTS _____	2 MIN
2	TGT 1 HIT _____ MISS _____ POINTS _____ TGT 2 HIT _____ MISS _____ POINTS _____	2 MIN
3	TGT 1 HIT _____ MISS _____ POINTS _____ TGT 2 HIT _____ MISS _____ POINTS _____	2 MIN
4	HIT _____ MISS _____ POINTS _____	2 MIN

TASK NUMBER	DAY AND NBC RECORD FIRE (CONT'D)	TIME
5	HIT _____ MISS _____ POINTS _____	2 MIN

TASK NUMBER	NIGHT RECORD FIRE	TIME
6	HIT _____ MISS _____ POINTS _____	2 MIN

TOTAL POINTS _____

EXPERT	80 – 90
GRENADIER, FIRST CLASS	70 – 75
GRENADIER, SECOND CLASS	60 – 65
UNQUALIFIED	0 – 55

GRADER'S SIGNATURE _____

OIC'S SIGNATURE _____

By Order of the Secretary of the Army:

ERIC K. SHINSEKI
General, United States Army
Chief of Staff

Official:

Joel B. Hudson

JOEL B. HUDSON
Administrative Assistant to the
Secretary of the Army
0307707

DISTRIBUTION:

Active Army, Army National Guard, and U. S. Army Reserve: To be distributed in accordance with the initial distribution number 110197, requirements for FM 3-22-31.